*This Classic Treasury
of Children's Prayers belongs to*

_____

_____

*The Classic Treasury
of Children's Prayers*

W e can do no great things,
Only small things with great love.

*Mother Teresa of Calcutta*

# The
# Classic
## Treasury
## of
# Children's
# Prayers

Compiled by
**Susan Cuthbert**

Illustrated by
**Alison Jay**

*Dedicated to everyone who prays with children,*
*and to Neil, Sharon and Rosalind—thanks*
*for all those sung graces! S.C.*

*To Maud and Johnny A.J.*

Compilation copyright © 1999 Susan Cuthbert
North American edition published 2000
by Augsburg Fortress, Publishers, Minneapolis
This edition copyright © 1999 Lion Publishing plc
Illustrations copyright © 1999 Alison Jay
Design by Nicky Farthing

ISBN 0-8066-4070-7
AF 9-4070
04 03 02 01 00   1 2 3 4 5 6 7 8 9 10

Typeset in 15/22 Venetian
Printed and bound in Singapore

# Contents

Introduction  8

A Wonderful World  11

The Changing Seasons  27

Creatures Great and Small  41

Here I Am  55

At Home  63

Bless Your People Everywhere  73

Now and For Ever  83

Christ Beside Me  91

Listening in the Stillness  107

Walking Tall  117

Forgiveness  129

Festivals  135

Blessings  151

Prayers from the Bible  173

Acknowledgments  205

Index of Themes  209

Index of Authors  219

Index of First Lines  220

# Introduction

Prayers are the expression of human understanding and hope. At the heart of Christian prayers lies a belief in a God who cares for this world, its creatures and its people; in a  God who is the Maker of all that is good and lovely, and who is more powerful than anything that threatens goodness and loveliness.

The prayers in this collection have been written at different times and in different places, yet each reveals a sincere faith in a loving God. Sometimes that faith is strong and confident; other times it is hesitant and uncertain, but for each writer, God is always there.

To read these prayers is to see the world through the eyes of faith; to wonder about life's mysteries; to explore its joys and sorrows and still trust that One who is greater than anything in this world is watching over all that happens and guiding the future.

# A Wonderful World

I will not hurry through this day!
Lord, I will listen by the way,
To humming bees and singing birds,
To speaking trees and friendly words;
And for the moments in between
Seek glimpses of thy great Unseen.

I will not hurry through this day;
I will take time to think and pray;
I will look up into the sky,
Where fleecy clouds and swallows fly:
And somewhere in the day, may be
I will catch whispers, Lord, from thee!

*Ralph Spaulding Cushman*

## Canticle of Brother Sun

O most high, almighty, good Lord, God:

to you belong praise, glory, honour and all blessing.

Praised be my Lord by all his creatures,

and chiefly by our brother the sun,

who brings us the day and the light.

Fair is he, and shines with a very great splendour:

O Lord, he points us to you.

Praised be my Lord by our sister the moon,

and by the stars which you have set clear and lovely in heaven.

Praised be my Lord by our brother the wind,

and by air and cloud, calms and all weather,

by which you uphold life in all creatures.

Praised be my Lord by our sister water,

who is very useful to us and humble and precious and clean.

Praised be my Lord by our brother fire,

through whom you give light in the darkness;

and he is bright and pleasant and very mighty and strong.

Praised be my Lord by our mother the earth,

who sustains us and keeps us,

and brings forth fruits of different kinds, flowers of many

colours, and grass.

*St Francis of Assisi (1181–1226)*

All things praise thee Lord most high!
Heaven and earth and sea and sky!

Time and space are praising thee!
All things praise thee; Lord, may we!

*George William Conder (1821–74)*

Thank you for the sunshine bright,
Thank you for the morning light.
Thank you for the rain and showers
Thank you for the fruit and flowers.
Thank you for each tall green tree
Thank you for the sand and sea.
Thank you for the winds that blow
Thank you for the frost and snow.
Thank you for the beasts so tall
Thank you for the creatures small.
Thank you for all things that live
Thank you, God, for all you give.

*H. Widdows*

Summer sky of blue and white,
Winter sky of grey;
Pink and orange in the dawnlight,
Red at close of day;
Noontime sun of golden yellow,
Moon with silver light:
Sing with gladness for the daytime,
Give thanks for the night.

*Mary Joslin*

i thank You God for most this amazing
day: for leaping greenly spirits of trees
and a blue true dream of sky; and for everything
which is natural which is infinite which is yes

(i who have died am alive again today,
and this is the sun's birthday; this is the birth
day of life and of love and wings: and of the gay
great happening illimitably earth)

how should tasting touching hearing seeing
breathing any—lifted from the no
of all nothing—human merely being
doubt unimaginable You?

(now the ears of my ears awake and
now the eyes of my eyes are opened)

*E.E. Cummings*

For flowers that bloom about our feet,
Father, we thank Thee,
For tender grass so fresh and sweet,
Father, we thank Thee,
For the song of bird and hum of bee,
For all things fair we hear or see,
Father in heaven, we thank Thee.

For blue of stream and blue of sky,
Father, we thank Thee,
For pleasant shade of branches high,
Father, we thank Thee,
For fragrant air and cooling breeze,
For beauty of the blooming trees,
Father in heaven, we thank Thee.

For this new morning with its light,
Father, we thank Thee,
For rest and shelter of the night,
Father, we thank Thee.
For health and food, for love and friends,
For everything thy goodness sends,
Father in heaven, we thank Thee.

*Ralph Waldo Emerson (1803–82)*

I look around and the sun's in the sky,
I look around and I think oh my!
The world is such a wonderful place.
And all because of the Good Lord's grace.

*Mary Batchelor*

For dawn of grey and tattered sky,
for silver rain on grass and tree;
for song and laughter and work well done,
our thankful hearts we raise to thee.

*Anonymous*

How did you make the rainbow,
And what is beyond the sky?
Why did you make the sun so hot,
And what makes the clouds race by?
You are the Lord, the Creator.
Only you know how and why.

*Elizabeth Laird*

Morning has broken
Like the first morning,
Blackbird has spoken
  Like the first bird.
Praise for the singing!
Praise for the morning!
Praise for them, springing
  From the first Word.

Sweet the rain's new fall
Sunlit from heaven,
Like the first dewfall
  In the first hour.
Praise for the sweetness
Of the wet garden,
Sprung in completeness,
  From the first shower.

Mine is the sunlight!
Mine is the morning
Born of the one light
  Eden saw play.
Praise with elation,
Praise every morning
Spring's re-creation
  Of the First Day!

*Eleanor Farjeon (1881–1965)*

## Morning Thanksgiving

Thank God for sleep in the long quiet night,
   For the clear day calling through the little leaded panes,
For the shining well-water and the warm golden light,
   And the paths washed white by singing rains.

For the treasure of the garden, the gilly-flowers of gold,
   The prouder petalled tulips, the primrose full of spring,
For the crowded orchard boughs, and the swelling buds that hold
   A yet unwoven wonder, to thee our praise we bring.

Thank God for good bread, for the honey in the comb,
   For the brown-shelled eggs, for the clustered blossom set
Beyond the open window in a pink and cloudy foam,
   For the laughing loves among the branches met.

For earth's little secret and innumerable ways,
   For the carol and the colour, Lord, we bring
What things may be of thanks, and that thou hast lent our days
   Eyes to see and ears to hear and lips to sing.

*John Drinkwater (1882–1936)*

## A Child's Prayer

For Morn, my dome of blue,
For Meadows green and gay,
And Birds who love the twilight of the leaves,
Let Jesus keep me joyful when I pray.

For the big Bees that hum
And hide in bells of flowers;
For the winding roads that come
To Evening's holy door,
May Jesus bring me grateful to his arms,
And guard my innocence for evermore.

*Siegfried Sassoon (1886–1967)*

The little cares that fretted me,
I lost them yesterday.
Among the fields above the sea,
Among the winds at play,
Among the lowing of the herds,
The rustling of the trees,
Among the singing of the birds,
The humming of the bees.

The foolish fears of what might pass
I cast them all away
Among the clover-scented grass
Among the new-mown hay,
Among the hushing of the corn
Where drowsy poppies nod,
Where ill thoughts die and good are born—
Out in the fields with God.

*Louise Imogen Guiney (1861–1920)*

Thank you, God in heaven
For a day begun.
Thank you for the breezes,
Thank you for the sun.
For this time of gladness,
For our work and play,
Thank you, God in heaven
For another day.

*Traditional*

## The Changing Seasons

Praise the Lord for all the seasons,
Praise Him for the gentle spring,
Praise the Lord for glorious summer,
Birds and beasts and everything.
Praise the Lord, who sends the harvest,
Praise Him for the winter snows,
Praise the Lord, all ye who love Him,
Praise Him, for all things he knows.

*Mary Anderson*

Praise the Lord for all the beauty
Coming with the blossoming spring.
Praise the Lord for summer showers;
Praise him for the birds that sing.
Praise the Lord for golden harvest,
Winter frost and white snowfall.
Praise him, praise him when December
Brings his Christmas festival.

*Elizabeth Gould (1900–84)*

Thank you very much indeed,
River, for your waving reed;
Hollyhocks, for budding knobs;
Foxgloves, for your velvet fobs;
Pansies, for your silky cheeks;
Chaffinches, for singing beaks;
Spring, for wood anemones
Near the mossy toes of trees;
Summer, for the fruited pear,
Yellowing crab, and cherry fare;
Autumn, for the bearded load,
Hazelnuts along the road;
Winter, for the fairy-tale,
Spitting log and bouncing hail.

But, blest Father, high above,
All these joys are from Thy love;
And Your children everywhere,
Born in palace, lane, or square,
Cry with voices all agreed,
'Thank you very much indeed.'

*Norman Gale*

Winter creeps,
Nature sleeps;
Birds are gone,
Flowers are none,
Fields are bare,
Bleak the air,
Leaves are shed:
All seems dead.

God's alive!
Grow and thrive.
Hidden away,
Bloom of May,
Robe of June!
Very soon
Nought but green
Will be seen!

*Percy Dearmer (1867–1936)*

How many miracles you strike in spring, Lord,
out of the hard winter's earth!

*Fiona Satow*

## Pippa's Song

The year's at the spring,
And day's at the morn;
Morning's at seven;
The hill-side's dew-pearled;
The lark's on the wing;
The snail's on the thorn:
God's in his heaven—
All's right with the world!

*Robert Browning (1812–89)*

Thank you, God, for sunshine,
Thank you, God, for spring,
Thank you, God, for sending
Every lovely thing.

*Mary Batchelor*

## Seaside

For buckets and spades, for sunshine and shade,
For sand in the toes, for cream on the nose,
For jumping the tide, for having a ride,
For laughter and fun, praise God every one.

*Christopher Herbert*

I'll shut my eyes and pretend I can be
Down by the side of the thundering sea,
Where the sea-gulls wheel on their great white wings,
And the wind shouts loud and the blown sand sings.

Thank You, Lord, that I'll soon be there,
Sand in my toes and wind in my hair,
While the sun burns hot in the high blue sky
And the big white clouds go marching by.

*Agnes Sanford*

## Water-ices

For water-ices, cheap but good,
That find us in a thirsty mood;
For ices made of milk or cream
That slip down smoothly as a dream;
For cornets, sandwiches and pies
That make the gastric juices rise;
For ices bought in little shops
Or at the kerb from him who stops;
For chanting of the sweet refrain:
'Vanilla, strawberry or plain?'
We thank thee Lord, who sendst with heat
This cool deliciousness to eat.

*Allen M. Laing*

For all the rich autumnal glories spread—
The flaming pageant of the ripening woods,
The fiery gorse, the heather-purpled hills;
The rustling leaves that fly before the wind
And lie below the hedgerows whispering;
For meadows silver-white with hoary dew;
The first crisp breath of wonder in the air,
We thank you, Lord.

*Anonymous*

We thank thee, Lord, for quiet upland lawns,
For misty loveliness of autumn dawns,
For gold and russet of the ripened fruit,
For yet another year's fulfilment, Lord,
  We thank Thee now.

For joy of glowing colour, flash of wings,
We thank Thee, Lord; for all the little things
That make the love and laughter of our days,
For home and happiness and friends, we praise
  And thank Thee now.

*Elizabeth Gould (1900–84)*

Thank you God for autumn days,
With shining fields and golden sheaves
And ripening fruits and rustling leaves;
For corn and flour and new-made bread,
And golden butter quickly spread.
Thank you for the friendly cow
Who gives us milk to make us grow;
For woolly sheep and clothing warm
To keep us all from cold and harm;
For nuts and fruits and berries red,
Upon the trees and bushes spread.
Man and child and beast and bird
Say, 'Thank you very much, dear God.'

*Mary Osborn*

First the seed
And then the grain;
Thank you, God,
For sun and rain.

First the flour
And then the bread;
Thank you, God,
That we are fed.

Thank you, God,
For all your care;
Help us all
To share and share.

*Lilian Cox*

Come, ye thankful people, come,
Raise the song of harvest-home!
All is safely gathered in,
Ere the winter storms begin;
God, our Maker, doth provide
For our wants to be supplied;
Come to God's own temple, come;
Raise the song of harvest-home!

*G.J. Elvey (1816–93)*

O thought I!
What a beautiful thing
God has made winter to be
by stripping the trees
and letting us see
their shapes and forms.
What a freedom does it seem
to give to the storms.

*Dorothy Wordsworth (1771–1855)*

We thank you, loving Father God
For things which warm us so;
For glowing fires and woolly gloves
Which make cold fingers glow;
For winter clothes and games to play
When we can skip and run...
And thank you for our cosy beds
When winter's day is done.

*Hilda I. Rostron*

# Creatures Great and Small

All things bright and beautiful,
All creatures, great and small,
All things wise and wonderful,
The Lord God made them all.

*Cecil Frances Alexander (1818–95)*

He prayeth best,
  Who loveth best
All things both great and small;
For the dear God
  Who loveth us,
He made and loveth all.

*Samuel Taylor Coleridge (1772–1834)*

Loving Father, hear my prayer,
For all your creatures everywhere;
For animals both big and small,
And for my pets—please bless them all.

*Mary Batchelor*

God bless the field and bless the furrow

Stream and branch and rabbit burrow...

Bless the minnow, bless the whale,

Bless the rainbow and the hail,

Bless the nest and bless the leaf,

Bless the righteous and the thief,

Bless the wing and bless the fin,

Bless the air I travel in,

Bless the mill and bless the mouse,

Bless the miller's bricken house,

Bless the earth and bless the sea,

God bless you and God bless me.

*Anonymous*

*The Prayer of the Little Ducks*

Dear God,

give us a flood of water.

Let it rain tomorrow and always.

Give us plenty of little slugs

and other luscious things to eat.

Protect all folk who quack

and everyone who knows how to swim.

Amen.

*Carmen Bernos de Gasztold*
*(translated from the French by Rumer Godden)*

W hen I see the birds go soaring,
wheeling, dipping through the sky,
Deep inside my spirit longs to
learn to fly.

*Lois Rock*

O nly a fool would fail
To praise God in his might
When the tiny mindless birds
Praise him in their flight.

*Anonymous (translated from the Irish by*
*Brendan Kennelly)*

I love God's tiny creatures
   That wander wild and free,
The coral-coated lady-bird,
   The velvet humming-bee;
Shy little flowers in hedge and dyke
   That hide themselves away;
God paints them, though they are so small,
   God makes them bright and gay.

*G.W. Briggs (1875–1959)*

God who has made the daisies
And every lovely thing,
He will accept our praises
And listen while we sing.

*Mary Batchelor*

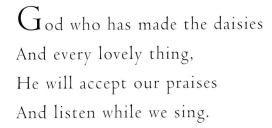

Please God, take care of little things,
The fledglings that have not their wings,
Till they are big enough to fly
And stretch their wings across the sky.

And please take care of little seeds
So small among the forest weeds
Till they have grown as tall as trees
With leafy boughs, take care of these.

And please take care of drops of rain
Like beads upon a broken chain,
Till in some river in the sun
The many silver drops are one.

Take care of small new lambs that bleat,
Small foals that totter on their feet,
And all small creatures ever known
Till they are strong to stand alone.

And please take care of children who
Kneel down at night to pray to you,
Oh please keep safe the little prayer
That like the big ones asks your care.

*Eleanor Farjeon (1881–1965)*

Praise God for the animals
for the colours of them,
for the spots and stripes of them,
for the patches and plains of them,
their claws and paws.

*Lynn Warren*

Like the ox that ploughs so straight
with slow and steady plod
May I learn the humble ways
to live as pleases God.

*Lois Rock*

$W$e pray, Lord, for the humble beasts who with us bear the burden and heat of the day, giving their lives for the well-being of their countries; and for the wild creatures, whom you have made wise, strong and beautiful; we ask for them your great tenderness of heart, for you have promised to save both man and beast, and great is your loving-kindness, O Saviour of the world.

*Russian prayer*

## *Prayer for Gentleness to All Creatures*

To all the humble beasts there be,

To all the birds on land and sea,

Great Spirit, sweet protection give

That free and happy they may live!

And to our hearts the rapture bring

Of love for every living thing;

Make us all one kin, and bless

Our ways with Christ's own gentleness!

*John Galsworthy (1867–1933)*

O heavenly Father, protect and bless
all things that have breath:
Guard them from all evil
and let them sleep in peace.

*Albert Schweitzer (1875–1965)*

# Here I Am

Dear Father, who hast all things made,
    And carest for them all,
There's none too great for thy great love,
    Nor anything too small;
If thou canst spend such tender care
    On things that grow so wild,
How wonderful thy love must be
    For me, thy little child.

*G.W. Briggs (1875–1959)*

My tongue can taste all sorts of things.
All kinds of things! So many things!
My nose can smell all sorts of things.
I thank you, Heavenly Father.

My ears can hear all sorts of things.
All kinds of things! So many things!
My eyes can see so many things.
I thank you, Heavenly Father.

My hands can touch all sorts of things.
All kinds of things! So many things!
And I can do so many things!
I thank you, Heavenly Father.

*Marjorie Newman*

Tennis racket, baseball bat,
rugby football, riding hat,
swimming costume, cricket stumps,
cycling helmet, skateboard jumps.
O Lord, for these and all our fun
we thank you each and every one.

*Christopher Herbert*

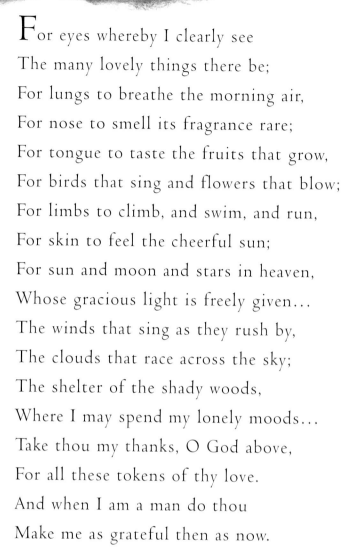

For eyes whereby I clearly see
The many lovely things there be;
For lungs to breathe the morning air,
For nose to smell its fragrance rare;
For tongue to taste the fruits that grow,
For birds that sing and flowers that blow;
For limbs to climb, and swim, and run,
For skin to feel the cheerful sun;
For sun and moon and stars in heaven,
Whose gracious light is freely given…
The winds that sing as they rush by,
The clouds that race across the sky;
The shelter of the shady woods,
Where I may spend my lonely moods…
Take thou my thanks, O God above,
For all these tokens of thy love.
And when I am a man do thou
Make me as grateful then as now.

*Richard Molesworth Dennis (died in 1914–18 war)*

God, who created me
Nimble and light of limb,
In three elements free,
To run, to ride, to swim,
Not when the sense is dim,
But now from the heart of joy,
I would remember Him:
Take the thanks of a boy.

*Henry Charles Beeching*

My body is paralysed.
By God's strength someday I will be free.
When that day comes I will be filled with joy.
   This I know.
I haven't walked from the day I was born,
On the warm backs of my parents and
brothers and sisters
I can go anywhere.
   This I know.
I am unable to speak.
I cannot speak gossip
Or speak harsh words.
   This I know.
In the midst of sorrow and pain
There is joy and happiness.
In the midst of this, I am alive.
   This I know.

*Kumi Hayashi*

I can do nothing
for my family
for people
or the Lord.
For the abundant love
of the Lord
of people
of my family
I just give thanks
just give thanks.

*Mizuno Genzo*

God, who made the earth,
The air, the sky, the sea,
Who gave the light its birth,
Careth for me.

God, who made the grass,
The flower, the fruit, the tree,
The day and night to pass,
Careth for me.

God, who made all things,
On earth, in air, in sea,
Who changing seasons bring,
Careth for me.

*Sarah Betts Rhodes (c. 1870)*

## At Home

We have so much to thank you for,
Our heavenly Father dear:
For life and love and tender care,
Through all the happy year;
For homes and friends and daily food,
Each one a gift of love.
For every good and perfect gift
Is from our God above.

*Mary Batchelor*

For every cup and plateful,
God make us truly grateful.

*A.S.T. Fisher*

God, we thank you for this food,
For rest and home and all things good;
For wind and rain and sun above,
But most of all for those we love.

*Maryleona Frost*

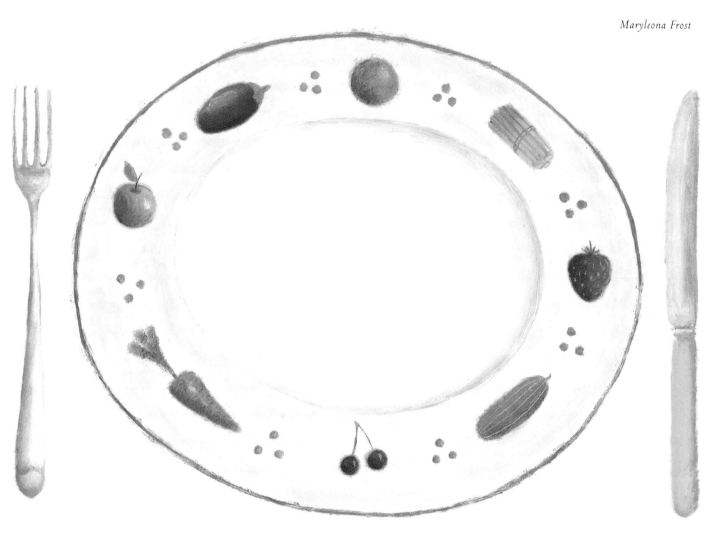

All good gifts around us
    Are sent from heaven above,
Then thank the Lord, O thank the Lord,
    For all his love.

*Matthias Claudius (1740–1815), translated by*
*Jane Montgomery Campbell (1817–78)*

Morning is here,
The board is spread,
Thanks be to God,
Who gives us bread.

*Anonymous*

We thank thee, Lord, for happy hearts,
For rain and sunny weather,
We thank thee, Lord, for this our food,
And that we are together.

*Emilie Fendall Johnson*

Thank you for the world so sweet,
Thank you for the food we eat,
Thank you for the birds that sing,
Thank you, God, for everything.

*Edith Rutter Leatham*

## The Miller's Grace

Back of the bread is the flour,
Back of the flour is the mill,
And back of the mill is the wind and the rain
And the Father's will.

*E.J. Allen-Williams*

## Johnny Appleseed Grace

The Lord is good to me,
And so I thank the Lord
For giving me the things I need,
The sun, the rain, the appleseed.
The Lord is good to me.

*Attributed to John Chapman, American pioneer*
*and planter of orchards (1774–1845)*

Blessed are you, Lord our God, King of the universe, who feeds the entire world in his goodness—with grace, with kindness and with mercy. He gives food to all life for his kindness is eternal… Blessed are you, God, who nourishes all.

*Jewish grace*

The bread is warm and fresh,
The water cool and clear.
Lord of all life, be with us,
Lord of all life, be near.

*African grace*

For health and strength
and daily food,
we praise your name,
O Lord.

*Traditional*

God is great, God is good,
Let us thank him for our food.

*Traditional, used in the White House
by President Jimmy Carter*

For our food and those who prepare it:
For health and friends to share it,
We thank You Lord.

*Anonymous*

For food and friends and all God sends,
We praise his holy name.

*E.J. Allen-Williams*

Be present at our Table, Lord,
Be here and everywhere adored;
Thy Creatures bless and grant that we
May feast in Paradise with Thee.

*John Cennick, Moravian deacon (1741)*

Us and this: God bless.

*Quaker grace*

Now my plate is full
But soon it will be gone
Thank you for my food
And please help those with none.

*Mike Brooks*

Some ha'e meat, and canna eat,
    And some wad eat that want it;
But we ha'e meat, and we can eat,
    And sae the Lord be thankit.

*Robert Burns (1759–96)*

Each time we eat,
May we remember God's love.

*Chinese grace*

Father of all mankind, make the roof of my house wide enough for all opinions, oil the door of my house so it opens easily to friend and stranger, and set such a table in my house that my whole family may speak kindly and freely around it. Amen.

*Prayer from Hawaii*

Let our friendships be strong, O Lord,
that they become a blessing to others...
Let our friendships be open, O Lord,
that they may be a haven for others...
Let our friendships be gentle, O Lord,
that they may bring peace to others...
for Jesus' sake. Amen.

*Christopher Herbert*

O God, help us not to despise or
oppose what we do not understand.

William Penn (1644–1718)

Put love into our hearts, Lord Jesus—
   love for you;
   love for those around us;
   love for all we find it hard to like.

Ena V. Martin

There are some old people whose lives
  are like autumn,
mellow, quiet and wise.
Help us, Lord, to admire them
and to listen to them patiently.

Christopher Herbert

Space counts for nothing, Lord, with thee;
Your love enfolds each family
Across the ocean, far away,
And here at home, where now we play,
And praise you for your care this day.

*Hilda I. Rostron*

May the love of God our Father
Be in all our homes today;
May the love of the Lord Jesus
Keep our hearts and minds always:
May his loving Holy Spirit
Guide and bless the ones I love,
Father, Mother, brothers, sisters,
Keep them safely in his love.

*Margaret Kitson*

## Bless Your People Everywhere

God of all our cities,
each alley, street, and square,
Please look down on every house
And bless the people there.

*Joan Gale Thomas*

When I call out, you will answer.

In fire and flood and danger,
In illness and sadness,
In war and in conflict,

When I call out, you will answer.

In hunger and thirst,
In ignorance and confusion,
In my need for shelter and warmth,

When I call out, you will answer.

God bless all those who are called
To work to help others in difficulty.
Thank you for giving them the strength
To do their jobs with courage and compassion.

When we call out, You will answer.

*Philip Tebbs*

Thank you for the firefighters. High above the ground, in the heat and smoke. Saving lives. Keep them safe, O Lord.

Thank you for the fishermen, their boats tossed by mighty waves and treacherous storms. Bring them home, O Lord.

Thank you for the doctors and nurses. Working through the night. Caring, tending. Comfort them, O Lord.

Thank you for all those who provide for us and give us what we need. Bless them and protect them, O Lord.

*Victoria Tebbs*

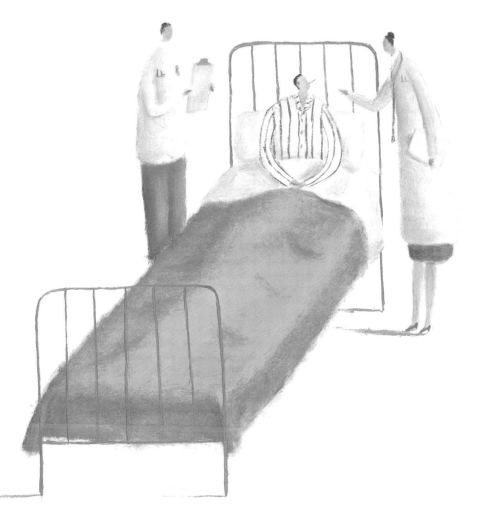

You are the God of the poor, the human and simple God, the God who sweats in the street, the God with a weather-beaten face. That's why I talk to you in the way that my people talk, because you are the labourer God, the worker Christ.

*From the Easter liturgy of a Catholic congregation in Nicaragua*

Wᴇ pray, mighty God, for those who struggle
that their life's flickering flame may not be snuffed out.
We pray for the poor and deprived,
for those exploited by the powerful and greedy,
and for a more human sharing of the plenty
you have given your world.

*Prayer from India*

Christ, let me see You in others,
Christ, let others see You in me.
Christ, let me see:

You are the caller,
You are the poor,
You are the stranger at my door.

You are the wanderer,
The unfed
You are the homeless
With no bed.

You are the man
Driven insane,
You are the child
Crying in pain.

You are the other who comes to me.
Open my eyes that I may see.

*David Adam*

O Great Spirit, help me never to
judge another until I have walked
two weeks in his moccasins.

*Prayer of the Sioux Indians*

Bless all the homeless ones
Near and far away,
And all the sad and lonely ones
Day by day.

And help us to remember them
Always in prayer,
And leave them, heavenly Father,
In your care.

*Dorothy E. Baker*

O Brother Jesus, who as a child was carried
   into exile,
Remember all those who are deprived of their
   home or country,
Who groan under the burden of anguish and
   sorrow,
Enduring the burning heat of the sun,
The freezing cold of the sea, or the humid
   heat of the forest,
Searching for a place of refuge.
Cause these storms to cease, O Christ.
Move the hearts of those in power
That they may respect the men and women
Whom you have created in your own image;
That the grief of refugees may be turned
   into joy.

*Prayer from Africa*

God our Father, Creator of the world,
please help us to love one another.
Make nations friendly with other nations;
make all of us love one another like
brothers and sisters.
Help us to do our part to bring peace in
the world
and happiness to all people.

*Prayer from Japan*

O Lord Jesus,
stretch forth your wounded hands
in blessing over your people,
to heal and restore,
and to draw them to yourself and
to one another in love.

*Prayer from the Middle East*

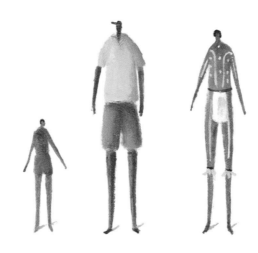

God our Father,
Who made us all,
Both rich and poor
And great and small,

And every race
Beneath the sun,
Please look after
Every one;

And teach us each
To love the rest,
For, North and South
And East and West,

Each of us
Belongs to thee,
And all the world's
Thy family.

*Joan Gale Thomas*

God bless Africa:
Guard her children,
Guide her rulers,
And give her peace,
For Jesus Christ's sake.

*Archbishop Trevor Huddleston*

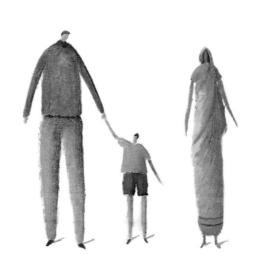

May your Holy Spirit brood
upon the islands of the world,
and bring peace, joy, and justice.

*Rajah Jacob*

## Now and For Ever

Be thou a bright flame before me,
Be thou a guiding star above me,
Be thou a smooth path below me,
Be thou a kindly shepherd behind me,
Today, tonight, and for ever.

*From* Carmina Gadelica

Jesus keep us
Safe to-day,
And keep all evil
Far away.

Watch my feet
In case I fall—
Let nothing frighten
Me at all,

And let my guardian
Angel be
Walking hand in hand
With me.

*Joan Gale Thomas*

Hear us, Holy Father,
As to you we pray,
Asking you to keep us
Safe from harm today.

*Traditional (adapted by Mike Brooks)*

Give me food that I may live;
Every naughtiness forgive:
Keep all evil things away
From Thy little child this day.

*William Canton*

Loving Shepherd of Thy sheep,
  Keep Thy lambs, in safety keep;
Nothing can Thy power withstand;
  None can pluck us from Thy hand.

*Jane Eliza Leeson (1807–82)*

Jesus, friend of little children,
  Be a friend to me;
Take my hand, and ever keep me
  Close to thee…

Never leave me, nor forsake me;
  Ever be my friend;
For I need thee, from life's dawning
  To its end.

*Walter John Mathams (1851–1931)*

Lord of all hopefulness, Lord of all joy,
Whose trust, ever child-like, no cares could destroy,
Be there at our waking, and give us, we pray,
Your bliss in our hearts, Lord, at the break of the day.

*Jan Struther (1901–53)*

I bind unto myself today
The power of God to hold and lead,
His eye to watch, his might to stay,
His ear to hearken to my need;
The wisdom of my God to teach,
His hand to guide, his shield to ward;
The word of God to give me speech,
His heavenly host to be my guard.

*St Patrick (389–461)*

God of the busy daytime;
God of the quiet night;
Whose peace pervades the darkness
And greets us with the light.
Safe with thy presence near us
Wherever we may be,
Thou, God, our great protector
We love and worship thee.

*John Oxenham (1852–1941)*

O Lord, thou knowest how busy I must be this day.
If I forget thee, do not thou forget me.

*Sir Jacob Astley (before the battle of Edgehill, 1642)*

Preserve us, O Lord, while waking
and guard us while sleeping;
that awake we may watch with Christ,
and asleep we may rest in peace.

*Traditional*

# Christit Beside Me

It is not far to go
for you are near.
It is not far to go,
for you are here.
And not by travelling, Lord,
we come to you,
but by the way of love,
and we love you.

*Amy Carmichael (1868–1951)*

O Christ, you calm the storm at sea;
  In tempest sore, be calming me.

O Christ, you walk upon the wave;
  When sinking fast, my footing save.

O Christ, the stricken child you raise;
  My spirit lift in joy and praise.

O Christ, you heal the man born blind;
  Make bright the darkness in my mind.

O Christ, you feed the crowd with bread;
  With words of truth let me be fed.

O Christ, you make the water wine;
  Take humble gifts and make them fine.

O Christ, the Resurrection Morn,
  With your new life my life adorn.

*Joyce Denham*

$Y$ou who guided Noah over the flood waves:

Hear us.

You who with your word recalled Jonah from the deep:

Deliver us.

You who stretched forth your hand to Peter as he sank:

Help us, O Christ.

Son of God, who did marvellous things of old:

Be favourable in our day also.

*Scots Celtic prayer*

O Jesus,
Be the canoe that holds me up
   in the sea of life;
Be the rudder that keeps me on
   a straight course;
Be the outrigger that supports
   me in times of great temptation.
Let your Spirit be my sail that
   carries me through each day.
Keep my body strong, so I can
   paddle steadfastly on in the
   voyage of life.

*Islander's prayer from Melanesia*

Dear God,
Be good to me,
The sea is so wide
And my boat is so small.

*Prayer of Breton fishermen*

Drive from me every
   temptation and danger,
Surround me on the sea
   of unrighteousness,
And in the narrows,
   crooks, and straits,
Keep thou my coracle,
   keep it always.

*From* Carmina Gadelica

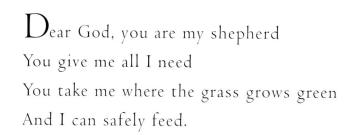

Dear God, you are my shepherd
You give me all I need
You take me where the grass grows green
And I can safely feed.

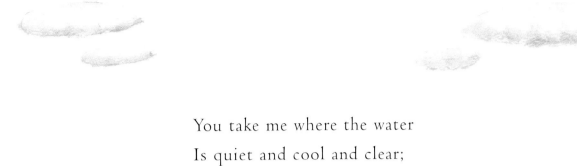

You take me where the water
Is quiet and cool and clear;
And there I rest and know I'm safe
For you are always near.

*Lois Rock (based on Psalm 23)*

As the rain hides the stars,
as the autumn mist hides the hills,
as the clouds veil the blue of the sky,
so the dark happenings of my lot
hide the shining of your face from me.
Yet, if I may hold your hand in the darkness,
it is enough. Since I know that, though
I may stumble in my going, you do not fall.

*Gaelic prayer (translated by Alistair MacLean)*

I believe in the sun even when it is
  not shining
I believe in love where feeling is not
I believe in God even if he is silent.

*Inscription on the walls of a cellar in Cologne,*
*Germany, where Jews hid from the Nazis*

God the Father, bless us,
God the Son, defend us,
God the Spirit, keep us
Now and evermore.

*Mary Batchelor*

Peace of the running waves to you,
Deep peace of the flowing air to you,
Deep peace of the quiet earth to you,
Deep peace of the shining stars to you,
Deep peace of the shades of night to you,
Moon and stars always giving light to you,
Deep peace of Christ, the Son of Peace, to you.

*Traditional Gaelic blessing*

Christ be with me
Christ within me
Christ behind me
Christ before me
Christ beside me
Christ to win me
Christ to comfort
and restore me

Christ beneath me
Christ above me
Christ in quiet and
Christ in danger
Christ in hearts of
all that love me
Christ in mouth of
friend and stranger.

*St Patrick (389–461)*

God, give me strength to run this race,
God, give me power to do the right,
And courage lasting through the fight;
God, give me strength to see thy face,
And heart to stand till evil cease,
And at the last, Oh God, thy peace.

*Jane Vansittart*

Nobody knows the trouble I see, nobody knows but Jesus.
Nobody knows the trouble I see, Glory Hallelujah!

Sometimes I'm up, sometimes I'm down, Oh yes, Lord!
Sometimes I'm almost to the groun', Oh yes, Lord.

Although you see me going along, Oh yes, Lord!
I have troubles here below, Oh yes, Lord.

What makes old Satan hate me so, Oh yes, Lord!
'Cause he got me once and let me go, Oh yes, Lord.

Nobody knows the trouble I see, nobody knows but Jesus.
Nobody knows the trouble I see, Glory Hallelujah!

*Black spiritual*

Jesus, who healed the sick,
Be with me in my pain;
Please help me to be brave
And make me well again.

*Mary Batchelor*

Lord, hang on to me,
because I don't feel well enough
to hang on to you.

*Angela Ashwin*

At even when the sun was set
    The sick, O Lord, around thee lay;
O, in what diverse pains they met!
    O with what joy they went away!

Once more 'tis eventide, and we
    Oppressed with various ills draw near;
What if thy form we cannot see?
    We know and feel that thou art here.

O Saviour Christ, our woes dispel;
    For some are sick, and some are sad,
And some have never loved thee well,
    And some have lost the love they had…

Thy touch has still its ancient power,
    No word from thee can fruitless fall;
Hear in this solemn evening hour,
    And in thy mercy heal us all.

*Henry Twells (1823–1900)*

Lord Jesus, you taught us to let the little
    children come to you,
and not to try to stop them;
into your loving hands we commend your child
for she is yours in death as in life.
Gather her to yourself gently, and in peace;
that she may be happy with you,
and, freed from all pain and fear,
may enjoy her new life for evermore.

*Written for the funeral of Eleanor, aged 6*

By and by all things must die,
We know this is so.
Animals, birds, the flowers, the trees,
People we love, those whose lives we share—
This is the hardest loss to bear.
When we are sad, Lord, you are there,
Loving and understanding.

*Alison Winn*

We give them back to you dear Lord,
who gavest them to us.
Yet as thou didst not lose them in giving,
so we have not lost them by their return.
For what is thine is ours always, if
We are thine.

*Quaker prayer*

Lead kindly light, amid the encircling gloom,

Lead thou me on;

The night is dark, and I am far from home;

Lead thou me on.

Keep thou my feet; I do not ask to see

The distant scene; one step enough for me.

*John Henry Newman (1801–90)*

## Listening in the Stillness

Come into my soul, Lord,
as the dawn breaks into the sky;
let your sun rise in my heart
at the coming of the day.

*Traditional*

The quiet room is hushed in prayer
We bow our heads while waiting here
And feel God's Spirit everywhere.

*Anonymous (adapted by Margaret Kitson)*

O let us feel you very near
When we kneel down to pray.
Let us be still that you may send
A message for today.

*Anonymous*

Still, very still.

Now I am ready for hearing God.

Now I am ready for listening.

Now I am ready to talk to him.

Still, very still.

*Anonymous*

Mountains are very still,
they just sit and sit and sit.
They point to your greatness, O God,
silent and quiet.
Help me to be still and silent,
like a mountain.
Sitting still, listening to your voice.

*Timothy King*

All is silent
In the still and soundless air,
I fervently bow
To my almighty God.

*Hsieh Ping-hsin, China*

Move our hearts with the calm,
smooth flow of your grace.
Let the river of your love run
through our souls. May my soul
be carried by the current of your
love, towards the wide, infinite
ocean of heaven.

*Gilbert of Hoyland (twelfth century)*

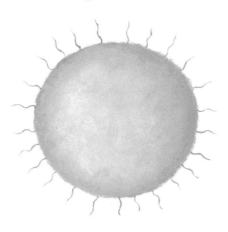

Here on the ancient rock of earth
I sit and watch the sky;
I feel the breeze that moves the trees
While stately clouds float by.
I wonder why our planet home
Spins round and round the sun
And what will last for ever
When earth's days all are done.

*Lois Rock*

O God, make us children of quietness,
and heirs of peace.

*St Clement of Alexandria (c. 150–215)*

# *Walking Tall*

I go forth today
in the might of heaven,
in the brightness of the sun,
in the whiteness of snow,
in the splendour of fire,
in the speed of lightning,
in the swiftness of wind,
in the firmness of rock.
I go forth today
in the hand of God.

*Eighth-century Irish prayer*

God, who touchest earth with beauty,
Make me lovely too;
With thy Spirit recreate me,
Make my heart anew.

Like thy springs and running waters,
Make me crystal pure;
Like thy rocks of towering grandeur,
Make me strong and sure.

Like thy dancing waves in sunlight,
Make me glad and free;
Like the straightness of the pine-trees
Let me upright be.

*Mary S. Edgar*

Thanks be to thee,
  O Lord Jesus Christ,
For all the benefits
  which thou hast won for us,
For all the pains and insults
  which thou hast borne for us.
O most merciful Redeemer,
Friend and Brother,
May we know thee more clearly,
  love thee more dearly,
  and follow thee more nearly,
  day by day.

*Richard of Chichester (1197–1253)*

Lord of the loving heart,
May mine be loving too,
Lord of the gentle hands,
May mine be gentle too.
Lord of the willing feet,
May mine be willing too,
So may I grow more like to thee
In all I say and do.

*Phyllis Garlick*

Jesus bids us shine
    With a pure, clear light,
Like a little candle
    Burning in the night;
In this world of darkness,
    So we must shine,
You in your small corner,
    And I in mine.

*Anonymous*

Let this day, O Lord, add some knowledge or good deed to yesterday.

*Lancelot Andrewes (1555–1626)*

The things, good Lord, that we pray for, give us grace to work for; through Jesus Christ our Lord.

*Thomas More (1478–1535)*

God be in my head, and in my understanding,
God be in mine eyes, and in my looking,
God be in my mouth, and in my speaking,
God be in my heart, and in my thinking,
God be at my end, and at my departing.

*Sarum Primer (1527)*

Lord Jesus Christ...
fill us with your love
that we may count nothing too
small to do for you,
nothing too much to give,
and nothing too hard to bear.

*St Ignatius Loyola (1491–1556)*

Teach us, Lord,
to serve you as you deserve,
to give and not to count the cost,
to fight and not to heed the wounds,
to toil and not to seek for rest,
to labour and not to ask for any reward
save that of knowing that we do your will.

*St Ignatius Loyola (1491–1556)*

We can do no great things,
Only small things with great love.

*Mother Teresa of Calcutta*

Lord, make me an instrument of your peace.

Where there is hatred, let me sow love;

Where there is injury, pardon;

Where there is discord, union;

Where there is doubt, faith;

Where there is despair, hope;

Where there is darkness, light;

Where there is sadness, joy.

O divine Master, grant that I may not
so much seek to be consoled, as to console,
to be understood, as to understand, to be
loved, as to love; for it is in giving that
we receive, it is in pardoning that we are
pardoned, and it is in dying that we are
born to eternal life.

*Attributed to St Francis of Assisi (1181–1226)*

I am only a spark
Make me a fire.
I am only a string
Make me a lyre.
I am only a drop
Make me a fountain.
I am only an ant hill
Make me a mountain.
I am only a feather
Make me a wing.
I am only a rag
Make me a king!

*Prayer from Mexico*

As our tropical sun gives forth its light,
so let the rays from your face enter every
nook of my being
and drive away all darkness within.

*Prayer from the Philippines*

O great Chief,
light a candle within my heart
that I may see what is therein
and sweep the rubbish from
your dwelling place.

*Prayer of an African girl*

You are to me, O Lord,
What wings are to the flying bird.

*Prayer from India*

## Forgiveness

Grandfather, look at our brokenness.
We know that in all creation only the human
family has strayed from the sacred way.
We know that we are the ones who are divided
and we are the ones who must come back
together to walk in the sacred way.
Grandfather, Sacred One,
teach us love, compassion and honour
that we may heal the earth and each other.

*Native American prayer, World Council of Churches*

Forgive me for the angry words
I didn't mean to say,
Forgive me for the fit of sulks
That spoiled a happy day.

Forgive me for the muddle
That I left upon the floor,
The tea I wouldn't eat,
The hasty way I slammed the door.

Forgive me for my selfishness
And all my little sins,
And help me to be better
When another day begins.

*Kathleen Partridge*

All that we ought to have thought and have not thought,
All that we ought to have said and have not said,
All that we ought to have done and have not done,
All that we ought not to have spoken and yet have spoken,
All that we ought not to have done, and yet have done,
For these words, and works, pray we, O God, for
forgiveness.

*Traditional*

Yoᴜ are wise and loving,
You are great and strong;
Glad when we do right,
Grieved when we do wrong.

Father God, our Father,
Guide us every hour;
Keep us safe and shield us
From temptation's power.

*Traditional (adapted by Mike Brooks)*

When I am tempted to take the sloping track
  of laziness,
the wide, flat street of greed and selfishness,
the thorn-lined way of anger and dislike,
the slippery cliff path of gossip and sharp words,
or the narrow alley of prejudice,
show me instead the high road of your kingdom.

*Susan Cuthbert*

Father, take all the broken bits of our lives

Our broken promises;

Our broken friendships;

Our differences of opinion,

Our different backgrounds, and shapes and sizes,

And arrange them together,

Fitting them into each other to make something
  beautiful

Like an artist makes a stained glass window.

Make a design

Your design

Even when all we can see are the broken bits.

*Anonymous*

For the things that I've done wrong,
Things that I remember long,
Hurting friends and those I love,
I am very sorry God.

*Norman and Margaret Mealey*

### *The Jesus Prayer*

Lord Jesus Christ,

Son of God,

have mercy on me a sinner!

*Traditional prayer of*
*Eastern Orthodox monks*

## Festivals

Harvest time is gold and red:
Thank you for our daily bread.
Christmas time is red and green:
Heaven now on earth is seen.
Easter time is green and white:
Bring us all to heaven's light.

*Lois Rock*

Let us thank God for Christmas:

For this happy and exciting time of the year
*Thank you loving Father.*

For Christmas trees and decorations
*Thank you loving Father.*

For cards and presents and good food
*Thank you loving Father.*

For fun with family and friends
*Thank you loving Father.*

For singing carols and listening to the
Christmas story
*Thank you loving Father.*

For all these things because we have them to
remind us of the coming of Jesus,
*Thank you loving Father.*

J.D. Searle

## *Just the Right Size*

We went to the beach, where the waves were so wild,
Much larger O Lord, than one little child;
I know we are small, but please, can you see,
Teddy bear, piglet, kitten and me?

We went to the zoo, where the elephants stay,
They're bigger than houses, too big to play;
I know we are small, but please, can you see,
Teddy bear, piglet, kitten and me?

We went to the woods, where the trees grow so high,
I can tell if I look, that they reach to the sky;
I know we are small, but please, can you see,
Teddy bear, piglet, kitten and me?

We've come to the stable, we followed the star,
Baby Jesus lies smiling, we know who you are—
You've made yourself small, so of course you can see,
Teddy bear, piglet, kitten and me!

*Catherine Maccabe*

Away in a manger, no crib for a bed,
The little Lord Jesus laid down his sweet head.
The stars in the bright sky looked down where he lay,
The little Lord Jesus asleep on the hay.

The cattle are lowing, the baby awakes,
But little Lord Jesus no crying he makes.
I love thee, Lord Jesus! Look down from the sky,
And stay by my side until morning is nigh.

Be near me, Lord Jesus; I ask thee to stay
Close by me for ever, and love me, I pray.
Bless all the dear children in thy tender care,
And fit us for heaven, to live with thee there.

*Traditional*

Thou didst leave thy throne and thy kingly crown
When thou camest to earth for me;
But in Bethlehem's home was there found no room
For thy holy Nativity:
O come to my heart, Lord Jesus;
There is room in my heart for thee.

*Emily E.S. Elliott*

## The Shepherd's Carol

We stood on the hills, Lady,
Our day's work done,
Watching the frosted meadows
That winter had won.

The evening was calm, Lady,
The air so still,
Silence more lovely than music
Folded the hill.

There was a star, Lady,
Shone in the night,
Larger than Venus it was
And bright, so bright.

Oh, a voice from the sky, Lady,
It seemed to us then
Telling of God being born
In the world of men.

And so we have come, Lady,
Our day's work done,
Our love, our hopes, ourselves
We give to your son.

*Clive Sansom*

What can I give him, poor as I am?
If I were a shepherd I would bring a lamb,
If I were a wise man I would do my part,—
Yet what I can I give him, give my heart.

*Christina Rossetti (1830–94)*

The Magi journeyed far to find
you, Redeemer and Saviour; we too
must search for you all our lives.
Help us to find you, Lord.

*Ianthe and Oliver Pratt*

God, our loving Father, help us remember the birth of Jesus, that we may share in the song of the angels, the gladness of the shepherds and the wisdom of the wise men.

Close the door of hate and open the door of love all over the world.

Let kindness come with every gift and good desires with every greeting.

Deliver us from evil by the blessing which Christ brings and teach us to be merry with clean hearts.

May the Christmas morning make us happy to be your children and the Christmas evening bring us to our beds with grateful thoughts, forgiving and forgiven, for Jesus' sake. Amen.

*Robert Louis Stevenson (1850–94)*

Who is this Jesus? Who can he be?
And what was the reason he came?
At Christmas we hear of a stable, a birth
And call to mind his name.

Who is this Jesus? Who can he be?
And what was the reason he came?
At Easter we hear how he died and then rose
And call to mind his name.

But what of the rest… of the land that he loved
Of the things that he spoke and the people he knew?
If we fill in the outline with colour and care
Will the real Jesus come into view?

Who is this Jesus? Who can he be?
And what was the reason he came?
Let's reflect on his story, his words and his deeds,
And call to mind his name.

*Sue Aldridge*

145

Blessed be the name of Jesus,
who died to save us.
Blessed be Jesus,
who had compassion on us.
Blessed be Jesus,
who suffered loneliness, rejection and pain,
for our sakes.
Blessed be Jesus,
through whose cross I am forgiven.
Lord Jesus, deepen my understanding
of your suffering and death.

*Written by young people in Kenya*

Christ is now risen again
From all his death and all his pain:
Therefore will we merry be,
And rejoice with him gladly. *Kyrieleison.**

Had he not risen again,
We had been lost, this is plain:
But since he is risen in deed,
Let us love him all with speed. *Kyrieleison.*

Now is a time of gladness,
To sing of the Lord's goodness:
Therefore glad now we will be,
And rejoice in him only. *Kyrieleison.*

*Miles Coverdale (1488–1568)*

* *Kyrieleison* (usually *Kyrie eleison*) is Greek for the prayer
'Lord, have mercy'.

The whole bright world rejoices now:
*with laughing cheer! with boundless joy!*
The birds do sing on every bough:
*Alleluia!*

Then shout beneath the racing skies:
*with laughing cheer! with boundless joy!*
To him who rose that we might rise:
*Alleluia!*

God, Father, Son and Holy Ghost:
*with laughing cheer! with boundless joy!*
Our God most high, our joy, our boast:
*Alleluia!*

*Easter carol (seventeenth century)*

Good Friday is a time of sadness,
Easter is a time of gladness.
On Good Friday Jesus died
But rose again at Eastertide.
All thanks and praise to God.

*Mary Batchelor*

## Blessings

Day is done,
Gone the sun
From the lake,
From the hills,
From the sky.
Safely rest,
All is well!
God is nigh.

*Anonymous*

Let the darkness of night surround us,
Let light and warmth gather us
And let God's people say Amen.
*Amen.*
Let the tools be stored away,
Let the work be over and done
And let God's people say Amen.
*Amen.*

Let the winds blow wild around us,
But let hearts be glad and minds be calm
And let God's people say Amen.
*Amen.*

*Ali Newell (from the Iona Community Worship Book)*

Now I lay me down to sleep,
I pray thee, Lord, thy child to keep;
Thy love to guard me through the night
And wake me in the morning light.

*Traditional*

Lord, keep us safe this night,
Secure from all our fears;
May angels guard us while we sleep,
Till morning light appears.

*John Leland (1754–1841)*

Now the daylight goes away,
Saviour listen while I pray.
Asking thee to watch and keep
And to send me quiet sleep.

Jesus, Saviour, wash away
All that has been wrong today:
Help me every day to be
Good and gentle, more like thee.

*Rev. W.H. Havergal (c. 1877)*

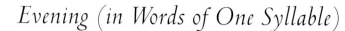

## Evening (in Words of One Syllable)

The day is past, the sun is set,
 And the white stars are in the sky;
While the long grass with dew is wet,
 And through the air the bats now fly.

The lambs have now lain down to sleep,
 The birds have long since sought their nests;
The air is still; and dark, and deep
 On the hill side the old wood rests.

Yet of the dark I have no fear,
 But feel as safe as when 'tis light;
For I know God is with me there,
 And He will guard me through the night.

For God is by me when I pray,
    And when I close mine eyes in sleep,
I know that He will with me stay,
    And will all night watch by me keep.

For He who rules the stars and sea,
    Who makes the grass and trees to grow,
Will look on a poor child like me,
    When on my knees I to Him bow.

He holds all things in His right hand,
    The rich, the poor, the great, the small;
When we sleep, or sit, or stand,
    Is with us, for He loves us all.

*Thomas Miller (1807–74)*

Now the day is over,
　　Night is drawing nigh;
Shadows of the evening
　　Steal across the sky.

Now the darkness gathers,
　　Stars begin to peep,
Birds and beasts and flowers
　　Soon will be asleep.

Jesus, give the weary
　　Calm and sweet repose;
With thy tenderest blessing
　　May our eyelids close.

Grant to little children
    Visions bright of thee;
Guard the sailors tossing
    On the deep blue sea.

Through the long night-watches
    May your angels spread
Their white wings above me,
    Watching over my bed.

When the morning wakens,
    Then may I arise,
Pure and fresh and sinless
    In thy holy eyes.

*Sabine Baring-Gould (1834–1924)*

Dear Jesus, as a hen covers her chicks
with her wings to keep them safe,
protect us this dark night under your
golden wings.

*Prayer from India*

## African Lullaby

Sleep my little one! The night is all wind and rain;

The meal has been wet by the raindrops

   and bent is the sugar cane;

O Giver who gives to the people,

   in safety my little son keep!

My little son with the head-dress, sleep, sleep, sleep!

*Traditional East African (translated by Holling C. Holling)*

Matthew, Mark, Luke, and John,
Bless the bed that I lie on.
Before I lay me down to sleep,
I pray the Lord my soul to keep.
Four corners to my bed,
Four angels there are spread,
Two at the foot, two at the head:
Four to carry me when I'm dead.
I go by sea, I go by land,
The Lord made me with His right hand.
Should any danger come to me,
Sweet Jesus Christ deliver me.
He's the branch and I'm the flower,
Pray God send me a happy hour,
And should I die before I wake,
I pray the Lord my soul to take.

*Traditional*

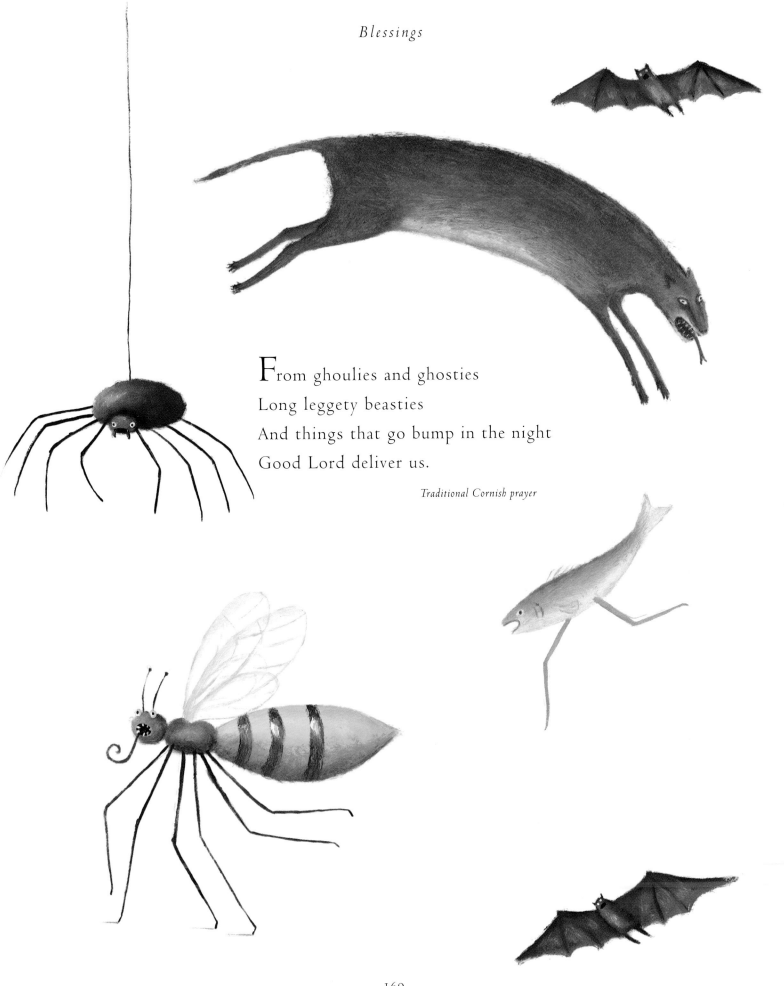

From ghoulies and ghosties
Long leggety beasties
And things that go bump in the night
Good Lord deliver us.

*Traditional Cornish prayer*

Peace be to this house
And to all who dwell in it.
Peace be to them that enter
And to them that depart.

*Anonymous*

Plenty of Grace
Be to this Place.

*Inscription on a
Tudor manor house*

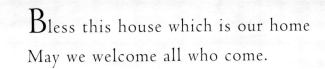

Bless this house which is our home
May we welcome all who come.

*Anonymous*

## *All Through the Night*

Sleep, my child, and peace attend thee,
All through the night;
Guardian angels God will send thee,
All through the night;
Soft the drowsy hours are creeping,
Hill and vale in slumber sleeping,
I my loving vigil keeping,
All through the night.

*Traditional Welsh prayer*

# Prayers from the Bible

Answer me now, Lord!
Remind me each morning of your
   constant love,
      for I put my trust in you.
My prayers go up to you;
      show me the way I should go.

*Psalm 143:7, 8*

Our Father, who art in heaven,
hallowed be thy name;
thy kingdom come;
thy will be done;
on earth as it is in heaven.
Give us this day our daily bread.
And forgive us our trespasses,
as we forgive those who trespass
   against us,
And lead us not into temptation;
but deliver us from evil.

For thine is the kingdom, the power,
   and the glory,
for ever and ever. Amen.

Our Father in heaven,
   hallowed be your name.
Your kingdom come.
Your will be done,
   on earth as it is in heaven.
Give us this day our daily bread.
And forgive us our debts,
   as we also have forgiven our debtors.
And do not bring us to the time of trial,
   but rescue us from the evil one.

*Matthew 6:9–13*

Praise the Lord!

Praise the Lord from heaven,
  you that live in the heights above.
Praise him, all his angels,
  all his heavenly armies.

Praise him, sun and moon;
    praise him, shining stars.
Praise him, highest heavens,
    and the waters above the sky.

Let them all praise the name of the Lord!
He commanded, and they were created;
    by his command they were fixed in
    their places for ever,
    and they cannot disobey.

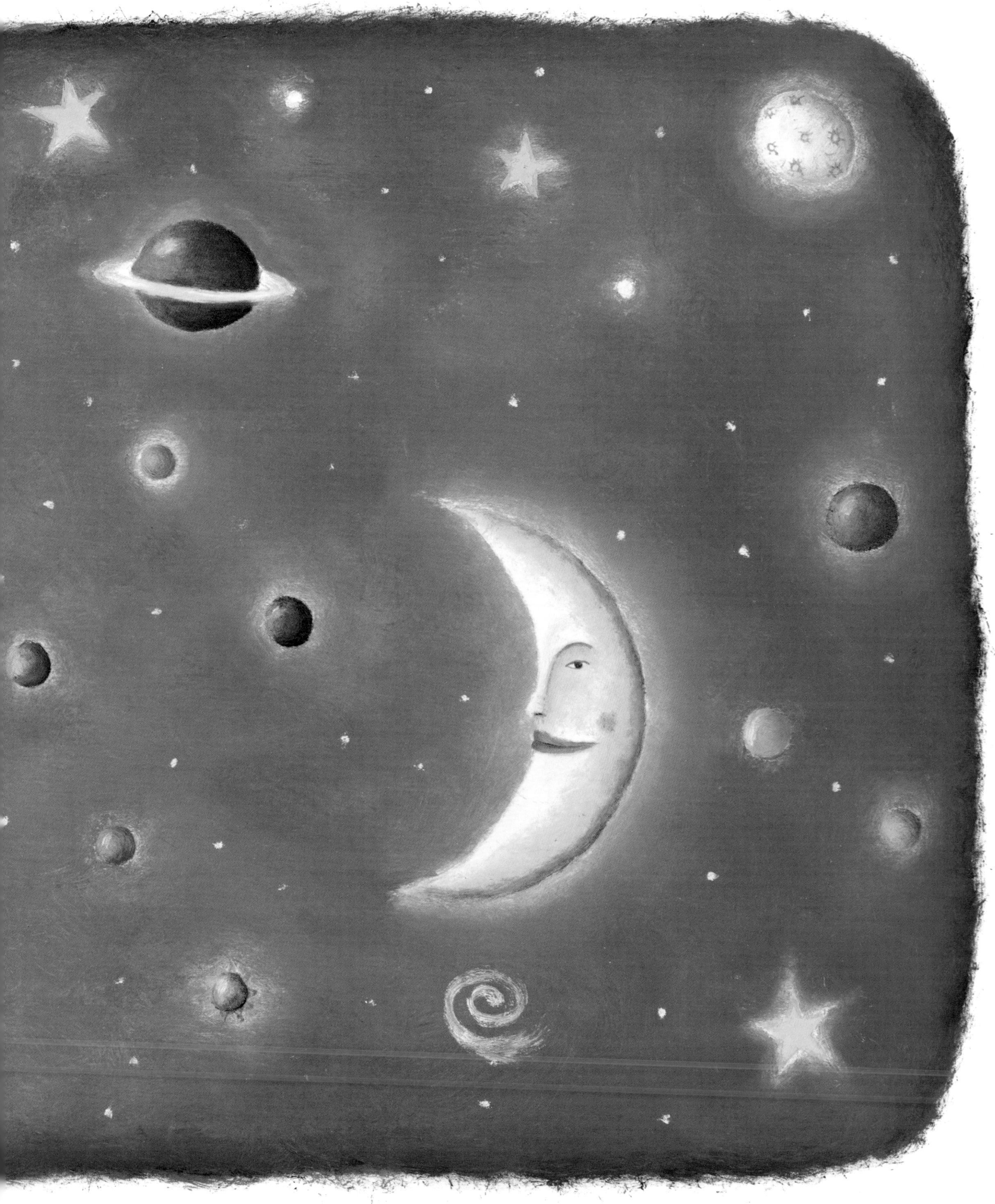

Praise the Lord from the earth,
  sea-monsters and all ocean depths;
lightning and hail, snow and clouds,
  strong winds that obey his command.

Praise him, hills and mountains,
   fruit-trees and forests;
all animals, tame and wild,
   reptiles and birds.

Praise him, kings and all peoples,
    princes and all other rulers;
girls and young men,
    old people and children too.

Let them all praise the name of the
    Lord!
His name is greater than all others;
    his glory is above earth and heaven.
He made his nation strong,
    so that all his people praise him—
    the people of Israel, so dear to him.

Praise the Lord!

*Psalm 148*

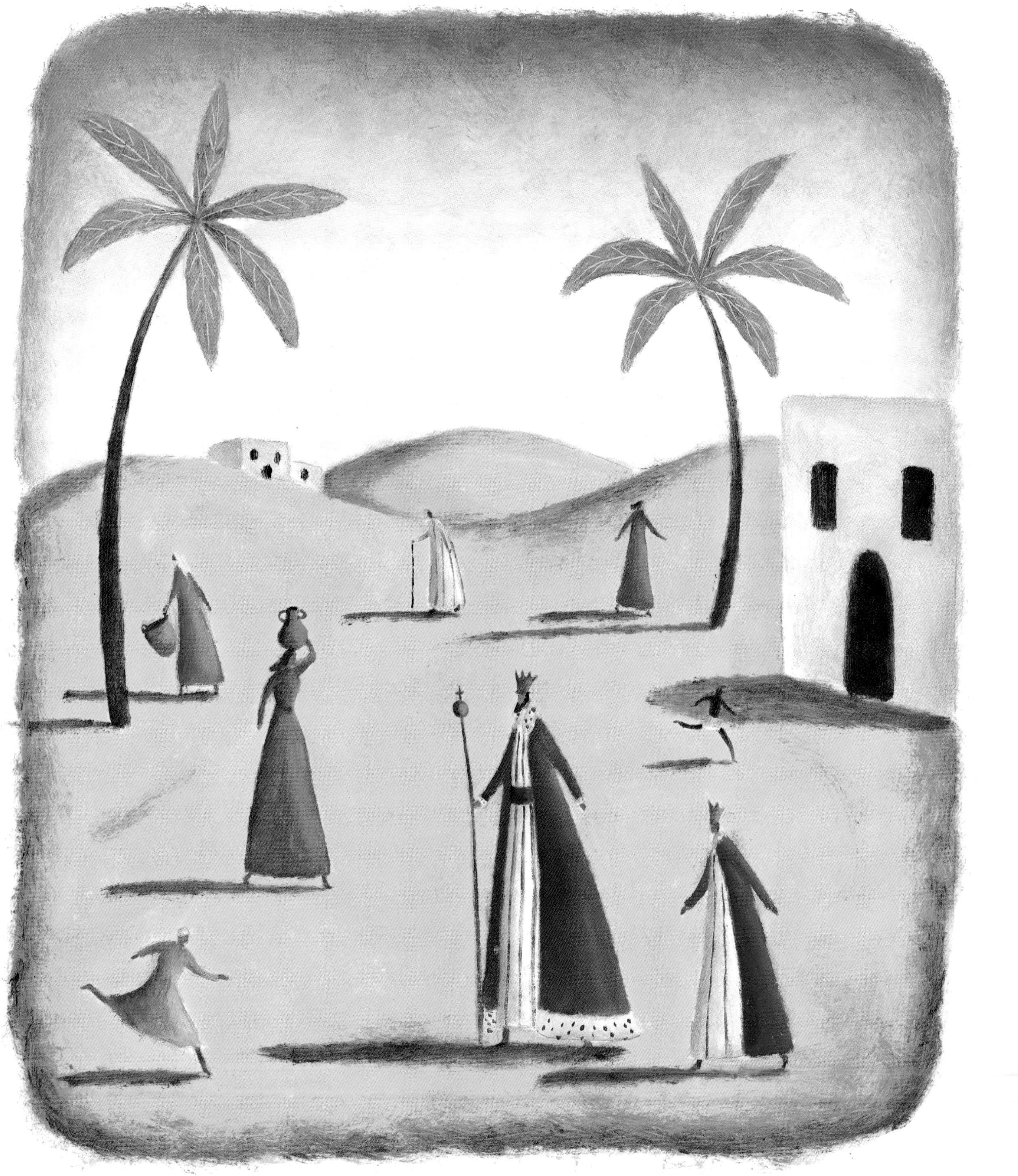

Praise the Lord!

Praise God in his Temple!
    Praise his strength in heaven!
Praise him for the mighty things
    he has done.
        Praise his supreme greatness.

Praise him with trumpets,
    Praise him with harps and lyres.
Praise him with drums and dancing
    Praise him with harps and flutes.
Praise him with cymbals.
    Praise him with loud cymbals.
Praise the Lord, all living creatures.

Praise the Lord!

*Psalm 150*

Sing a new song to the Lord!
Sing to the Lord, all the world!
Sing to the Lord, and praise him!

*Psalm 96:1–2*

O Lord, my Lord,

how great you are in all the world.

Your glory reaches higher than the sky;

you call forth praises even from children and babies,

and shut the mouths of your enemies.

When I look at the heavens,

the work of your fingers,

the moon and the stars that you set in their places,

who am I that you should think of me?

Why should you care for human beings?

Yet you made us just a little lower than the angels,

and crowned us with blessing.

You gave us the power to rule over all that you have made:

flocks and herds,

all the animals of the field,

the birds of the air,

even the fish that swim in the seas.

O Lord, my Lord,

how great you are in all the world.

*Psalm 8 (adapted by Susan Cuthbert)*

How great and wonderful are all your works,
   Lord God Almighty;
upright and true are all your ways,
   King of nations.
Who does not revere and glorify your name, O Lord?
For you alone are holy,
   and all nations will come and adore you
   for the many acts of saving justice you have shown.

*Revelation 15:3–4*

## *A Prayer for Help*

How much longer will you forget me, Lord?
  For ever?
How much longer will you hide yourself from me?
How long must I endure trouble?
How long will sorrow fill my heart day and night?
How long will my enemies triumph over me?

Look at me, O Lord my God, and answer me.
  Restore my strength; don't let me die.
Don't let my enemies say, 'We have defeated him.'
  Don't let them gloat over my downfall.

I rely on your constant love;
  I will be glad, because you will rescue me.
I will sing to you, O Lord,
  because you have been good to me.

*Psalm 13*

Create a pure heart in me, O God,
  and put a new and loyal spirit in me.
Do not banish me from your presence;
  do not take your holy spirit away from me.
Give me again the joy that comes from
  your salvation,
  and make me willing to obey you.

*Psalm 51:10–12*

Ever since I was a child,

you loved me.

You called me;

but the more you called to me,

the more I turned away from you.

Yet you were the one who taught me to walk.

You took me up in your arms,

but I did not acknowledge that you took care of me.

You drew me to you with affection and love.

You picked me up and held me to your cheek.

You bent down to me and fed me.

Yet I insisted on turning away from you.

And now I cry out:

Do not give me up! Do not abandon me!

For you are God and not a human being.

I pray that you, the Holy One, will always be with me.

*Hosea 11:1–9 (adapted by Philip Law)*

Lord, I have given up my pride
  and turned away from my arrogance.
I am not concerned with great matters
  or with subjects too difficult for me.
  Instead, I am content and at peace.
As a child lies quietly in its mother's arms,
  so my heart is quiet within me.

*Psalm 131:1–2*

The Lord is my light and my salvation;
 I will fear no one.
The Lord protects me from all danger;
 I will never be afraid.

*Psalm 27:1*

How I love you, Lord!
   You are my defender.

The Lord is my protector;
   he is my strong fortress.
My God is my protection,
   and with him I am safe.
He protects me like a shield;
   he defends me and keeps me safe.
I call to the Lord,
   and he saves me from my enemies.
Praise the Lord!

*Psalm 18:1–3*

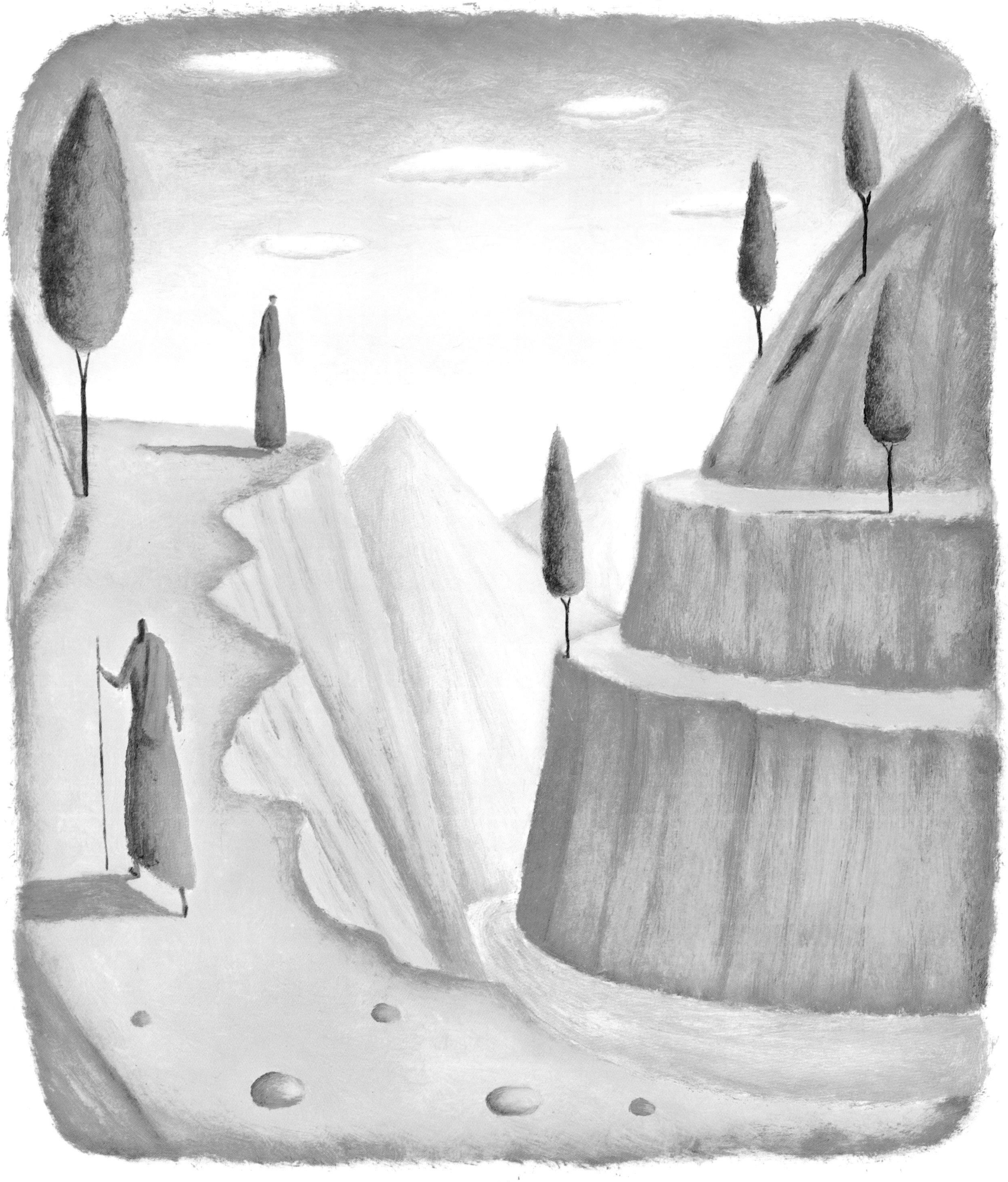

I look to the mountains;
  where will my help come from?
My help will come from the Lord,
  who made heaven and earth.

He will not let you fall;
  your protector is always awake.

The protector of Israel
  never dozes or sleeps.
The Lord will guard you;
  he is by your side to protect you.
The sun will not hurt you during the day,
  nor the moon during the night.

The Lord will protect you from all danger;
  he will keep you safe.
He will protect you as you come and go
  now and for ever.

*Psalm 121*

## *Magnificat*

My soul magnifies you, my Lord,
  and my spirit rejoices in God my Saviour,
    for you have looked with favour on the lowliness of your servant.
You, the Mighty One, have done great things for me,
  and holy is your name.
Your mercy is for those who fear you from generation to generation.
You have scattered the proud in the thoughts of their hearts.
You have brought down the powerful from their thrones,
  and lifted up the lowly;
You have filled the hungry with good things,
  and sent the rich away empty.

*Luke 1:46–55 (adapted by Philip Law)*

I pray for the gift of love;
  for if I have not love, I am nothing.
Teach me, in love, to be patient and kind;
  not envious, boastful or conceited.
Never let me be rude, selfish or quick to take offence;
  may I keep no score of wrongs.
Never let me take pleasure in the sins of others;
  may I take delight in the truth.
For then there will be nothing my love cannot face;
  no limit to its faith, its hope, its endurance.
My love will never end.

*1 Corinthians 13:2, 4–8 (adapted by Philip Law)*

Dear Father,
Help us to love one another
with the love that comes from you.
For we know that everyone who loves is your child,
but whoever fails to love does not know you,
because you are love.
You revealed your love for us
by sending your only Son into the world
that we might have life through him.

Dear Father, if you loved us so much,
we too should love one another.
No one has ever seen you,
but as long as we love one another
you remain in us
and your love comes to its perfection in us.

*1 John 4:7–14 (adapted by Philip Law)*

The Lord bless thee,
and keep thee:
The Lord make his face shine upon thee,
and be gracious unto thee:
The Lord lift up his countenance upon thee,
and give thee peace.

*Numbers 6:24–26*

When I lie down, I go to sleep
in peace;
you alone, O Lord, keep me
perfectly safe.

*Psalm 4:8*

May the grace of the Lord Jesus
Christ, and the love of God, and
the fellowship of the Holy Spirit
be with us all, evermore.

*Based on 2 Corinthians 13:14 ('The Grace')*

# Acknowledgments

Thanks go to all those who have given permission to include material in this book, as indicated in the list below. Every effort has been made to trace and contact copyright owners. We apologize for any inadvertent omissions or errors.

'Christ, let me see You in others' by **David Adam** from *The Cry of the Deer*. Reprinted by permission of SPCK and Morehouse Publishing. 'Who is this Jesus? Who can he be?' by **Sue Aldridge**. Used by permission of Chris Chesterton. 'The Miller's Grace' and 'For food and friends and all God sends' by **E.J. Allen-Williams** from *A Book of Graces*, compiled by Carolyn Martin, published by WI Books Ltd and Hodder and Stoughton Ltd. Reprinted by permission. 'Praise the Lord for all the seasons' by **Mary Anderson** from *A Year of Prayers*, reprinted by permission of World International Ltd. Copyright © 1992 World International Ltd. 'Lord, hang on to me' by **Angela Ashwin**, from *Prayer in the Shadows*, published in 1990 by HarperCollins *Publishers* Ltd. 'Bless all the homeless ones' by **Dorothy E. Baker** from *Praise Him*, compiled by M. Grace Bartlett, published in 1959 by the Church Information Office. 'I look around and the sun's in the sky' by **Mary Batchelor** from *The Lion Book of Bible Stories and Prayers*, published in 1980 by Lion Publishing plc. 'God who has made the daisies', 'Thank you, God, for sunshine', 'Loving Father, hear my prayer', 'God the Father, bless us', 'Jesus, who healed the sick' and 'We have so much to thank you for' by Mary Batchelor from *My Own Book of Prayers*, published in 1984 by Lion Publishing plc. 'Good Friday is a time of sadness' by Mary Batchelor from *The Lion Prayer Collection*, published in 1992 by Lion Publishing plc. Reprinted by permission of William Neill-Hall Ltd. Extracts from 'I love God's tiny creatures' by **G.W. Briggs** from *Songs of Praise for Boys and Girls* by permission of Oxford University Press (1929). 'Now my plate is full' by **Mike Brooks**, and 'Hear us, Holy Father' and 'You are wise and loving' adapted by Mike Brooks, from *A Year of Prayers* by Mike Brooks, reprinted by permission of World International Ltd. Copyright © 1992 World International Ltd. 'Give me food that I may live' by **William Canton** from *A Patchwork of Blessings and Graces* compiled by Mary Daniels, published jointly in 1996 by Gracewing and Peake Road. Reprinted by permission. 'It is not far to go' by **Amy Carmichael** from *Edges of His Ways*. Reprinted by permission of the Christian Literature Crusade, Fort Washington, PA, USA, and edited. 'First the seed' by **Lilian Cox** from *New Child Songs*. Reprinted by permission of the National Christian Education Council. 'i thank You God for most this amazing day' is reprinted from *Complete Poems 1904–1962*, by **E.E. Cummings**, edited by George James Firmage, by permission of W.W. Norton and Company, copyright © 1991 by the Trustees for the E.E. Cummings Trust and George James Firmage. 'When I am tempted', copyright © 1999 **Susan Cuthbert**. 'Winter creeps' by **Percy Dearmer** from *Songs of Praise*, copyright © 1931 Oxford University Press. Reprinted by permission. 'For Help and Protection', copyright © 1998 Joyce Denham from *A Child's Book of Celtic Prayers*, published in 1998 by Lion Publishing plc. Reprinted by permission. 'Morning Thanksgiving' by **John Drinkwater** from *The Collected Poems of John Drinkwater Vol. I, 1908–1917*, reprinted by permission of Samuel French Ltd on behalf of the Estate of John Drinkwater. 'Morning has broken' by **Eleanor Farjeon** from *The Children's Bells*, published by Oxford University Press and 'A Prayer for Little Things' by Eleanor Farjeon from *Silver, Sand and Snow*, published by Michael Joseph. Reprinted by permission of David Higham Associates Ltd. 'For every cup and plateful' by **A.S.T. Fisher** from *A Patchwork of Blessings and Graces* compiled by Mary Daniels, published jointly in 1996 by Gracewing and Peake Road. Reprinted by permission. 'Table Blessing' by **Maryleona Frost** from *Poems and Prayers for the Very Young*, published in 1973 by Random House. 'Prayer for gentleness to all creatures' by **John Galsworthy** from *Collected Poems*. Reprinted by permission of The Society of Authors as the Literary Representative of the Estate of John Galsworthy. 'Lord of the loving heart' by **Phyllis Garlick** from *All Our Days* by Irene Taylor and Phyllis Garlick, published by the Church Mission Society. 'The Prayer of the Little Ducks' by **Carmen Bernos de Gasztold** from *Prayers from the Ark*, translated by Rumer Godden, copyright © 1962, 1963 Rumer Godden. Reprinted by permission of Macmillan Children's Books, London (UK rights), Curtis Brown (US rights) on behalf of Rumer Godden. 'I can do nothing' by **Mizuno Genzo** from *Pocket Prayers*, compiled by Christopher Herbert, published in 1993, 1998 by Church House Publishing. 'Grace and Thanksgiving' by **Elizabeth Gould** from *Come Follow Me*, published by HarperCollins *Publishers* Ltd. Reprinted by permission. 'My body is paralysed' by **Kumi Hayashi** from *Oceans of Prayer* compiled by Maureen Edwards and Jan S. Pickard, published in 1991 by the National Christian Education Council. Reprinted by permission. 'Seaside', 'Sport', 'Let our friendships be strong, O Lord' and 'Old people' by **Christopher Herbert** from *The Prayer Garden—An Anthology of Children's Prayers*, compiled by Christopher Herbert, published by HarperCollins *Publishers* Ltd. Reprinted by permission. 'All is silent' by **Hsieh Ping-hsin** from *Your Will be Done*, published by CCA Youth, Hong Kong. 'God bless Africa' by **Archbishop Trevor Huddleston** from *The Prayer Garden—An Anthology of Children's Prayers*, compiled by Christopher Herbert, published by HarperCollins *Publishers* Ltd. Reprinted by permission. 'May your Holy Spirit brood' by **Rajah Jacob** from *Oceans of Prayer* compiled by Maureen Edwards and Jan S. Pickard, published in 1991 by the National Christian Education Council. Reprinted by permission. 'Summer sky of blue and white' by **Mary**

**Joslin**, copyright © 1999, Lion Publishing plc. 'God's Praises' translated by **Brendan Kennelly** from *The Penguin Book of Irish Verse*, introduced and edited by Brendan Kennelly, published in 1970 by Penguin Books, copyright © 1970 Brendan Kennelly. 'How did you make the rainbow' by **Elizabeth Laird** from *Prayers for Children* compiled by Christopher Herbert, published by HarperCollins *Publishers* Ltd. Reprinted by permission. Bible extracts adapted by **Philip Law** from *A Time to Pray*, copyright © 1997 Lion Publishing plc. 'Thank you for the world so sweet' by **Edith Rutter Leatham** from *Further Everyday Prayers*, published by the National Christian Education Council. Reprinted by permission. 'We went to the beach, where the waves were so wild', copyright © 1999 **Catherine Maccabe**. 'Jesus, friend of little children' by **Walter John Mathams** from *Prayers and Hymns for Little Children*, published by Oxford University Press. Reprinted by permission. 'For the things that I've done wrong' by **Norman and Margaret Mealey** from *Sing for Joy*. Reprinted by permission of the Domestic and Foreign Missionary Society of the Protestant Episcopal Church USA. 'Let the darkness of night surround us' by **Ali Newell** from the 'Creation Liturgy' from the *Iona Community Worship Book*, published in 1991 by Wild Goose Publications, Glasgow. 'My tongue can taste all sorts of things' by **Marjorie Newman** from *A Year of Prayers*, compiled by Mike Brooks, copyright © 1992 World International Publishing Ltd. 'Autumn Days' by **Mary Osborn** from *Good and Gay*, published by SPCK. 'The Magi journeyed far to find you' from *A Litany for Epiphany*, copyright © **Ianthe and Oliver Pratt**. Reprinted by permission. 'Dear God, you are my shepherd', 'Harvest time is gold and red', 'Here on the ancient rock of earth', 'Like the ox that ploughs so straight' and 'When I see the birds go soaring' by **Lois Rock**, copyright © 1999 Lion Publishing plc. 'We thank you, loving Father God' by **Hilda I. Rostron** from *New Child Songs*, published by the National Christian Education Council. Reprinted by pemission. 'Space counts for nothing, Lord, with thee' by Hilda I. Rostron from *Missionary Prayers and Praises*, published by the National Christian Education Council. Reprinted by permission. 'Seaside' by **Agnes Sanford** from *Let's Believe*, published by Arthur James Ltd. Reprinted by permission. 'The Shepherds' Carol' by **Clive Sansom** from *The Witnesses and other poems*, published by Methuen. Reprinted by permission of David Higham Associates Ltd. 'A Child's Prayer' by **Siegfried Sassoon** from *Collected Poems*. Reprinted by permission of George Sassoon. 'O heavenly Father, protect and bless' by **Albert Schweitzer**, from *Prayers for Children* compiled by Inga Moore, copyright © 1988 Grisewood and Dempsey. Reprinted by permission. 'Lord of all hopefulness, Lord of all joy' by **Jan Struther** from *Enlarged Songs of Praise*, published in 1931 by Oxford University Press. Reprinted by permission. 'When I call out, you will answer', copyright © 1999 **Philip Tebbs**. 'Thank you for the firefighters', copyright © 1999 **Victoria Tebbs**. 'God of all our cities' by **Joan Gale Thomas** from *God of all Things*, published by A.R. Mowbray & Co. 'God our Father, who made us all' and 'Jesus keep us safe to-day' by Joan Gale Thomas from *Our Father*, published by A.R. Mowbray & Co. Reprinted by permission of Deborah Sheppard. 'Thank you for the sunshine bright' by **H. Widdows** from *In Excelsis*, compiled by H.W. Dobson, published in 1962 by the Church Information Office. Reprinted by permission. 'Guard me by day' by **Elfreyda M.C. Wightman** from *Stories of Jesus for Mothers to Tell*, published by The Lutterworth Press. Reprinted by permission.

**Miscellaneous**
'For dawn of grey and tattered sky' (p. 18), 'Morning is here' (p. 64) and 'God is great, God is good' (p. 68) from *A Book of Graces*, compiled by Carolyn Martin, published by WI Books Ltd and Hodder and Stoughton Ltd. Reprinted by permission. 'For our food and those who prepare it' (p. 68), 'Us and this: God bless' (p. 68) and 'Plenty of Grace' (p. 170) from *A Patchwork of Blessings and Graces* by Mary Daniels, published jointly in 1996 by Gracewing and Peake Road. Reprinted by permission. 'Father of all mankind' (p. 70) from *Another Day* by John Carden, published in 1986 by Triangle/SPCK. Reprinted by permission. 'You are the God of the poor' (p. 76) from the Easter liturgy of a Catholic congregation in Managua from *Oceans of Prayer* compiled by Maureen Edwards and Jan S. Pickard, published in 1991 by the National Christian Education Council. Reprinted by permission. 'O Great Spirit' (p. 78) from *Book of Childhood Prayers and Verses* compiled by Carolyn Martin, copyright © 1983 Hodder and Stoughton. Reprinted by permission. 'O Brother Jesus' (p. 79) and 'Come into my soul, Lord' (p. 107) from *The Book of a Thousand Prayers*, compiled by Angela Ashwin, published by HarperCollins *Publishers* Ltd. Reprinted by permission. 'O Lord Jesus, stretch forth your wounded hands' (p. 80) from *Morning, Noon and Night*, edited by John Carden, published in 1976 by the Church Missionary Society. Reprinted by permission. 'Be thou a bright flame before me' (p. 83) and 'Drive from me every temptation and danger' (p. 95) from 'The guardian angel' from *Carmina Gadelica*, Vol. I, collected by Alexander Carmichael, published by Scottish Academic Press, 1928. Reprinted by permission. 'Preserve us, O Lord, while waking' (p. 90) from *The Prayer Book as Proposed in 1928* and reproduced in *Lent, Holy Week and Easter* is copyright © The Central Board of Finance of the Church of England 1984, 1986 and is reproduced by permission. 'Still, very still' (p. 109) from *Growing Up*, edited by Vivyen Bremner, published by the National Society and SPCK. Reprinted by

permission. 'I am only a spark' (p. 126) from *Prayers for Mission*, copyright © USPG. 'Grandfather, look at our brokenness' (p. 129) from the World Council of Churches Consultation, quoted in the IAMS newsletter. Reprinted from *Oceans of Prayer* by permission of the National Christian Education Council. Extract from 'Blessed be the name of Jesus' (p. 146) by the young people in Kenya from *Pray with Us*, compiled by Maureen Edwards, published by Lion Publishing plc. 'Sleep my little one!' (p. 166) translated by Holling C. Holling from *My Book House* copyright © The United Educators, Inc. Used by permission. 'Our Father, who art in heaven' (p. 174) from *The Alternative Service Book 1980*, copyright © The Central Board of Finance of the Church of England. Reprinted by permission.

**Use of Bible translations**

Extract on p. 202 from the Authorized Version of the Bible (The King James Bible), the rights in which are vested in the Crown, is reprinted by permission of the Crown's Patentee, Cambridge University Press. Extracts on pp. 173, 176, 186, 187, 190, 191, 193, 194, 195, 197 and 203 from the Good News Bible, published by Bible Societies/HarperCollins Publishers Ltd, UK, copyright © American Bible Society, New York 1966, 1971, 1976, 1992. Extract on p. 189 from The New Jerusalem Bible, published and copyright © 1985 by Darton, Longman and Todd Ltd and Doubleday and Co. Inc. Extract on p. 175 from The New Revised Standard Version of the Bible, Anglicized Edition, copyright © 1989, 1995 by the Division of Christian Education of the National Council of the Churches of Christ in the United States of America, is used by permission. All rights reserved.

# Index of Themes

**air**
O most high, almighty, good Lord, God   12
For flowers that bloom about our feet   17
God bless the field and bless the furrow   44
For eyes whereby I clearly see   58
God, who made the earth   62

**animals**
Praise the Lord for all the seasons   27
Thank you God for autumn days   36
All things bright and beautiful   41
Loving Father, hear my prayer   43
God bless the field and bless the furrow   44
Dear God, give us a flood of water   44
I love God's tiny creatures   46
Please God, take care of little things   48
Praise God for the animals   50
Like the ox that ploughs so straight   50
We pray, Lord, for the humble beasts   51
To all the humble beasts there be   52
By and by all things must die   105
The day is past, the sun is set   160
Now the day is over   162
Praise the Lord! Praise the Lord from heaven   176

**autumn**
Thank you very much indeed   29
For all the rich autumnal glories spread   34
We thank thee, Lord, for quiet upland lawns   35
Thank you God for autumn days   36
There are some old people whose lives are like autumn   71

**babies**
Sleep, my child, and peace attend thee   172

**birds**
Morning has broken   20
The year's at the spring   31
I'll shut my eyes and pretend I can be   32
God bless the field and bless the furrow   44
Dear God, give us a flood of water   44
When I see the birds go soaring   45
Only a fool would fail   45
Please God, take care of little things   48
To all the humble beasts there be   52
By and by all things must die   105
You are to me, O Lord   128
The day is past, the sun is set   160
Now the day is over   162
Dear Jesus, as a hen covers her chicks   164

**Christmas**
Harvest time is gold and red   135
Let us thank God for Christmas   136
We went to the beach, where the waves were so wild   137
Away in a manger, no crib for a bed   138
Thou didst leave thy throne and thy kingly crown   139
We stood on the hills, Lady   140
What can I give him   142
The Magi journeyed far to find you   142
God, our loving Father, help us remember the birth of Jesus   143

## death

Winter creeps   30
Jesus, friend of little children   85
I believe in the sun even when it is not shining   98
Lord Jesus, you taught us to let the little children come to you   104
By and by all things must die   105
We give them back to you, dear Lord   105
God be in my head, and in my understanding   122

## disaster

When I call out, you will answer   74
Thank you for the firefighters   75
How much longer will you forget me, Lord?   190

## earth

O most high, almighty, good Lord, God   12
All things praise thee Lord most high!   13
i thank You God for most this amazing   16
God bless the field and bless the furrow   44
God, who made the earth   62
Peace of the running waves to you   99
Here on the ancient rock of earth   115
Grandfather, look at our brokenness   129
Harvest time is gold and red   135
Praise the Lord! Praise the Lord from heaven   176

## Easter

Harvest time is gold and red   135
Who is this Jesus? Who can he be?   145
Blessed be the name of Jesus   146
Christ is now risen again   148
The whole bright world rejoices now   149
Good Friday is a time of sadness   150

## evening

Summer sky of blue and white   15
For Morn, my dome of blue   24
At even when the sun was set   103
We stood on the hills, Lady   140
God, our loving Father, help us remember the birth of Jesus   143
Jesus, tender Shepherd, hear me   158
Now the daylight goes away   159
Now the day is over   162

## family

To all the humble beasts there be   52
My body is paralysed   60
I can do nothing   61
Space counts for nothing, Lord, with thee   72
May the love of God our Father   72
God our Father, Creator of the world   80
God our Father, who made us all   81
Let us thank God for Christmas   136

## fearfulness

The little cares that fretted me   25
Dear Father, who hast all things made   55
When I call out, you will answer   74
Be thou a bright flame before me   83
Jesus keep us safe to-day   84
Hear us, Holy Father   84
Give me food that I may live   84
Loving Shepherd of Thy sheep   85
Jesus, friend of little children   85
I bind unto myself today   86
God of the busy daytime   88
Preserve us, O Lord, while waking   90
O Christ, you calm the storm at sea   92
You who guided Noah over the flood waves   93
O Jesus, be the canoe that holds me up in the sea of life   95
Dear God, be good to me   95
Drive from me every temptation and danger   95
As the rain hides the stars   98
I believe in the sun even when it is not shining   98
God, give me strength to run this race   101

Lord Jesus, you taught us to let the little children come
  to you 104
Lead kindly light, amid the encircling gloom 106
Lord, keep us safe this night 154
The day is past, the sun is set 160
From ghoulies and ghosties 169
The Lord is my light and my salvation 194

## food

For water-ices, cheap but good 33
We thank thee, Lord, for quiet upland lawns 35
Thank you God for autumn days 36
First the seed 37
Come, ye thankful people, come 37
For eyes whereby I clearly see 58
God, who made the earth 62
We have so much to thank you for 63
For every cup and plateful 64
God, we thank you for this food 64
Morning is here 64
We thank thee, Lord, for happy hearts 65
Thank you for the world so sweet 65
Back of the bread is the flour 66
The Lord is good to me 66
Blessed are you, Lord our God 67
The bread is warm and fresh 67
For health and strength 67
God is great, God is good 68
For our food and those who prepare it 68
For food and friends and all God sends 68
Be present at our Table, Lord 68
Us and this: God bless 68
Now my plate is full 69
Some ha'e meat, and canna eat 69
Each time we eat 69

Give me food that I may live 84
Harvest time is gold and red 135
Let us thank God for Christmas 136
Our Father, who art in heaven 174
Our Father in heaven 175

## forgiveness

O God, help us not to despise 71
Put love into our hearts, Lord Jesus 71
At even when the sun was set 103
God, who touchest earth with beauty 118
As our tropical sun gives forth its light 127
O great Chief, light a candle within my heart 127
Grandfather, look at our brokenness 129
Forgive me for the angry words 130
All that we ought to have thought and have not thought 130
Father, take all the broken bits of our lives 133
For the things that I've done wrong 133
Lord Jesus Christ, Son of God 134
God, our loving Father, help us remember the birth
  of Jesus 143
Glory to Thee, my God, this night 156
Ah, dearest Jesus, holy Child 158
Jesus, tender Shepherd, hear me 158
Now the daylight goes away 159
Our Father, who art in heaven 174
Our Father in heaven 175
Create a pure heart in me, O God 191
Ever since I was a child 192

## friends

For flowers that bloom about our feet 17
We thank thee, Lord, for quiet upland lawns 35
We have so much to thank you for 63
For our food and those who prepare it 68
For food and friends and all God sends 68
Father of all mankind, make the roof of my house 70
Let our friendships be strong, O Lord 70
Jesus, friend of little children 85
For the things that I've done wrong 133
Let us thank God for Christmas 136
Jesus, tender Shepherd, hear me 158

## games

Thank you, God in heaven for a day begun 26
For buckets and spades, for sunshine and shade 32
We thank you, loving Father God 40
Tennis racket, baseball bat 57
For eyes whereby I clearly see 58
God, who created me 59

## graces

We have so much to thank you for   63
For every cup and plateful   64
God, we thank you for this food   64
All good gifts around us   64
Morning is here   64
We thank thee, Lord, for happy hearts   65
Thank you for the world so sweet   65
Back of the bread is the flour   66
The Lord is good to me   66
Blessed are you, Lord our God   67
The bread is warm and fresh   67
For health and strength   67
God is great, God is good   68
For our food and those who prepare it   68
For food and friends and all God sends   68
Be present at our Table, Lord   68
Us and this: God bless   68
Now my plate is full   69
Some ha'e meat, and canna eat   69
Each time we eat   69
Father of all mankind, make the roof of my house   70

## harvest

Praise the Lord for all the seasons   27
Praise the Lord for all the beauty   28
Thank you God for autumn days   36
First the seed   37
Come, ye thankful people, come   37
Harvest time is gold and red   135

## holidays

For buckets and spades, for sunshine and shade   32
I'll shut my eyes and pretend I can be   32

## home

We thank thee, Lord, for quiet upland lawns   35
We have so much to thank you for   63
Father of all mankind, make the roof of my house   70

May the love of God our Father   72
God of all our cities   73
Bless all the homeless ones   79
O Brother Jesus, who as a child was carried into exile   79
Here on the ancient rock of earth   115
Peace be to this house   170
Plenty of Grace   170
Bless this house which is our home   171

## hopes and ambitions

When I see the birds go soaring   45
Like the ox that ploughs so straight   50
O God, help us not to despise   71
I bind unto myself today   86
God, give me strength to run this race   101
Thanks be to thee, O Lord Jesus Christ   119
Lord of the loving heart   120
Let this day, O Lord   121
The things, good Lord, that we pray for   121
God be in my head, and in my understanding   122
Lord Jesus Christ... fill us with your love   123
Teach us, Lord, to serve you as you deserve   123
We can do no great things   4, 124
Lord, make me an instrument of your peace   124
I am only a spark   126
As our tropical sun gives forth its light   127
We stood on the hills, Lady   140
The Magi journeyed far to find you   142
Create a pure heart in me, O God   191
I pray for the gift of love   200

## illness

My body is paralysed   60
When I call out, you will answer   74
Christ, let me see You in others   78
O Lord Jesus, stretch forth your wounded hands   80
O Christ, you calm the storm at sea   92
Jesus, who healed the sick   102
Lord, hang on to me   102
At even when the sun was set   103
Lord Jesus, you taught us to let the little children come to you   104

## journeys

I go forth today   117
The Magi journeyed far to find you   142

## justice

My body is paralysed   60
You are the God of the poor   76

We pray, mighty God, for those who struggle   77
Christ, let me see You in others   78
O Great Spirit, help us never to judge another   78
O Brother Jesus, who as a child was carried into exile   79
May your Holy Spirit brood   82
Lord, make me an instrument of your peace   124
Our Father, who art in heaven   174
Our Father in heaven   175
How great and wonderful are all your works   189
My soul magnifies you, my Lord   198

## light

O most high, almighty, good Lord, God   12
Thank you for the sunshine bright   14
Summer sky of blue and white   15
Morning has broken   20
Thank God for sleep in the long quiet night   22
For eyes whereby I clearly see   58
God, who made the earth   62
God of the busy daytime   88
Lead kindly light, amid the encircling gloom   106
Jesus bids us shine   121
Lord, make me an instrument of your peace   124
As our tropical sun gives forth its light   127
Harvest time is gold and red   135
Let the darkness of night surround us   152
Now I lay me down to sleep   154
Lord, keep us safe this night   154
Guard me by day   155
Jesus, tender shepherd, hear me   158
The day is past, the sun is set   160
The Lord is my light and my salvation   194

## loneliness

For eyes whereby I clearly see   58
Bless all the homeless ones   79
Blessed be the name of Jesus   146
How much longer will you forget me, Lord?   190

## love

Thank you very much indeed   29
We thank thee, Lord, for quiet upland lawns   35
He prayeth best   42
To all the humble beasts there be   52
Dear Father, who hast all things made   55
I can do nothing   61
We have so much to thank you for   63
God, we thank you for this food   64
All good gifts around us   64
Each time we eat   69
Put love into our hearts, Lord Jesus   71
Space counts for nothing, Lord, with thee   72
May the love of God our Father   72
God our Father, Creator of the world   80
O Lord Jesus, stretch forth your wounded hands   80
God our Father, who made us all   81
It is not far to go   91
I believe in the sun even when it is not shining   98
Move our hearts with the calm   112
Lord of the loving heart   120
Lord Jesus Christ... fill us with your love   123
We can do no great things   124
Lord, make me an instrument of your peace   124
Grandfather, look at our brokenness   129
We stood on the hills, Lady   140
God, our loving Father, help us remember the birth of Jesus   143
God bless all those that I love   155
Sleep, my child, and peace attend thee   172
Answer me now, Lord!   173
How much longer will you forget me, Lord?   190
Ever since I was a child   192
I pray for the gift of love   200
Dear Father, help us to love one another   201
May the grace of the Lord Jesus Christ   203

## morning

Summer sky of blue and white   15
For flowers that bloom about our feet   17
For dawn of grey and tattered sky   18
Morning has broken   20
Thank God for sleep in the long quiet night   22
For Morn, my dome of blue   24
Thank you, God in heaven for a day begun   26
The year's at the spring   31
For eyes whereby I clearly see   58
Morning is here   64
Lord of all hopefulness, Lord of all joy   86
Come into my soul, Lord   107
Answer me now, Lord!   173

## natural world

I will not hurry through this day!   11
O most high, almighty, good Lord, God   12
All things praise thee Lord most high!   13
Thank you for the sunshine bright   14
Summer sky of blue and white   15
i thank You God for most this amazing day   16
For flowers that bloom about our feet   17
I look around and the sun's in the sky   18
For dawn of grey and tattered sky   18
How did you make the rainbow   19
Morning has broken   20
Thank God for sleep in the long quiet night   22
For Morn, my dome of blue   24
The little cares that fretted me   25
Thank you, God in heaven for a day begun   26
Praise the Lord for all the seasons   27
Praise the Lord for all the beauty   28
Thank you very much indeed   29
Winter creeps   30
How many miracles you strike in spring, Lord   30
The year's at the spring   31
Thank you, God, for sunshine   31
I'll shut my eyes and pretend I can be   32
For all the rich autumnal glories spread   34
We thank thee, Lord, for quiet upland lawns   35
Thank you God for autumn days   36
O thought I!   38
All things bright and beautiful   41
God bless the field and bless the furrow   44
Dear God, give us a flood of water   44
I love God's tiny creatures   46
God who has made the daisies   47
Please God, take care of little things   48
For eyes whereby I clearly see   58
God, who made the earth   62

By and by all things must die   105
Here on the ancient rock of earth   115
God, who touchest earth with beauty   118

## night-time

Summer sky of blue and white   15
For flowers that bloom about our feet   17
Thank God for sleep in the long quiet night   22
God, who made the earth   62
Thank you for the firefighters   75
God of the busy daytime   88
Away in a manger, no crib for a bed   138
Day is done   151
Let the darkness of night surround us   152
Now I lay me down to sleep   154
Lord, keep us safe this night   154
Guard me by day   155
Glory to Thee, my God, this night   156
Jesus, tender shepherd, hear me   158
The day is past, the sun is set   160
Now the day is over   162
Dear Jesus, as a hen covers her chicks   164
Sleep my little one! The night is all wind and rain   166
From ghoulies and ghosties   169
Sleep, my child, and peace attend thee   172
How much longer will you forget me, Lord?   190
I look to the mountains   197

## old people

There are some old people whose lives are like autumn   71

## peace

I will not hurry through this day!   11
We thank thee, Lord, for quiet upland lawns   35
O heavenly Father, protect and bless   54
Let our friendships be strong, O Lord   70
God our Father, Creator of the world   80
God bless Africa   81
May your Holy Spirit brood   82
God of the busy daytime   88
Preserve us, O Lord, while waking   90
Peace of the running waves to you   99
God, give me strength to run this race   101
Lord Jesus, you taught us to let the little children come
    to you   104
The quiet room is hushed in prayer   108
O let us feel you very near   108
Still, very still   109
Mountains are very still   110
All is silent   111
Move our hearts with the calm   112
O God, make us children of quietness   116
We stood on the hills, Lady   140
Glory to Thee, my God, this night   156
Ah, dearest Jesus, holy Child   158
The day is past, the sun is set   160
Now the day is over   162
Peace be to this house   170
Sleep, my child, and peace attend thee   172
Lord, I have given up my pride   193
The Lord bless thee   202
When I lie down, I go to sleep in peace   203

## poverty

Now my plate is full   69
When I call out, you will answer   74
You are the God of the poor   76
We pray, mighty God, for those who struggle   77
Christ, let me see You in others   78
Bless all the homeless ones   79
O Brother Jesus, who as a Child was carried into exile   79
God our Father, who made us all   81
The Magi journeyed far to find you   142
My soul magnifies you, my Lord   198

## praise

O most high, almighty, good Lord, God   12
All things praise thee Lord most high!   13
Summer sky of blue and white   15
Morning has broken   20
Praise the Lord for all the seasons   27
Praise the Lord for all the beauty   28
How many miracles you strike in spring, Lord   30
For buckets and spades, for sunshine and shade   32
We thank thee, Lord, for quiet upland lawns   35
Come, ye thankful people, come   37
All things bright and beautiful   41
Only a fool would fail   45
God who has made the daisies   47
Praise God for the animals   50
We have so much to thank you for   63
For health and strength   67
Space counts for nothing, Lord, with thee   72
O Christ, you calm the storm at sea   92
Christ is now risen again   148
The whole bright world rejoices now   149
Good Friday is a time of sadness   150
Glory to Thee, my God, this night   156
Praise the Lord! Praise the Lord from heaven   176
Praise the Lord! Praise God in his Temple!   186
Sing a new song to the Lord!   187
O Lord, my Lord, how great you are in all the world   188
How much longer will you forget me, Lord?   190
How I love you, Lord!   195
My soul magnifies you, my Lord   198

## protection and safety

For flowers that bloom about our feet   17
For Morn, my dome of blue   24
Thank you God for autumn days   36
Dear God, give us a flood of water   44
Please God, take care of little things   48
To all the humble beasts there be   52
O heavenly Father, protect and bless   54

Dear Father, who hast all things made   55
The bread is warm and fresh   67
Space counts for nothing, Lord, with thee   72
May the love of God our Father   72
God of all our cities   73
When I call out, you will answer   74
Thank you for the firefighters   75
Bless all the homeless ones   79
God our Father, who made us all   81
God bless Africa   81
Be thou a bright flame before me   83
Jesus keep us safe to-day   84
Hear us, Holy Father   84
Give me food that I may live   84
Loving Shepherd of Thy sheep   85
Jesus, friend of little children   85
Lord of all hopefulness, Lord of all joy   86
I bind unto myself today   86
God of the busy daytime   88
O Lord, thou knowest how busy I must be this day   89
Preserve us, O Lord, while waking   90
O Christ, you calm the storm at sea   92
You who guided Noah over the flood waves   93
O Jesus, be the canoe that holds me up in the sea of life   95
Dear God, be good to me   95
Drive me from every temptation and danger   95
As the rain hides the stars   98
I believe in the sun even when it is not shining   98
God the Father, bless us   99
Christ be with me   100
God, give me strength to run this race   101
Lord, hang on to me   102
Lead kindly light, amid the encircling gloom   106
O let us feel you very near   108
I go forth today   117
You are to me, O Lord   128
You are wise and loving   131
When I am tempted to take the sloping track of laziness   132
Away in a manger, no crib for a bed   138

Now I lay me down to sleep   154
Lord, keep us safe this night   154
Guard me by day   155
Jesus, tender Shepherd, hear me   158
Now the daylight goes away   159
The day is past, the sun is set   160
Now the day is over   162
Dear Jesus, as a hen covers her chicks   164
Sleep my little one! The night is all wind and rain   166
Matthew, Mark, Luke, and John   168
From ghoulies and ghosties   169
Sleep, my child, and peace attend thee   172
Our Father, who art in heaven   174
Our Father in heaven   175
How much longer will you forget me, Lord?   190
Ever since I was a child   192
The Lord is my light and my salvation   194
How I love you, Lord!   195
I look to the mountains   197
My soul magnifies you, my Lord   198
The Lord bless thee   202
When I lie down, I go to sleep in peace   203

## sadness

My body is paralysed   60
I can do nothing   61
When I call out, you will answer   74

Bless all the homeless ones   79
O Brother Jesus, who as a child was carried into exile   79
Nobody knows the trouble I see, nobody knows but Jesus   101
At even when the sun was set   103
By and by all things must die   105
How much longer will you forget me, Lord?   190

## special people
God, we thank you for this food   64
When I call out, you will answer   74
Thank you for the firefighters   75
God bless all those that I love   155

## spring
Morning has broken   20
Thank God for sleep in the long quiet night   22
Praise the Lord for all the seasons   27
Praise the Lord for all the beauty   28
Thank you very much indeed   29
Winter creeps   30
How many miracles you strike in spring, Lord   30
The year's at the spring   31
Thank you, God, for sunshine   31

## summer
I will not hurry through this day!   11
Summer sky of blue and white   15
Praise the Lord for all the seasons   27
Praise the Lord for all the beauty   28
Thank you very much indeed   29
Winter creeps   30
For buckets and spades, for sunshine and shade   32
I'll shut my eyes and pretend I can be   32
For water-ices, cheap but good   33

## thanksgiving
Thank you for the sunshine bright   14
Summer sky of blue and white   15
i thank You God for most this amazing day   16
For flowers that bloom about our feet   17
For dawn of grey and tattered sky   18
Thank God for sleep in the long quiet night   22
For Morn, my dome of blue   24
Thank you, God in heaven for a day begun   26
Thank you very much indeed   29
Thank you, God, for sunshine   31
I'll shut my eyes and pretend I can be   32
For water-ices, cheap but good   33
For all the rich autumnal glories spread   34
We thank thee, Lord, for quiet upland lawns   35
Thank you God for autumn days   36

First the seed   37
Come, ye thankful people, come   37
We thank you, loving Father God   40
My tongue can taste all sorts of things   56
Tennis racket, baseball bat   57
For eyes whereby I clearly see   58
God, who created me   59
I can do nothing   61
We have so much to thank you for   63
For every cup and plateful   64
God, we thank you for this food   64
All good gifts around us   64
Morning is here   64
We thank thee, Lord, for happy hearts   65
Thank you for the world so sweet   65
The Lord is good to me   66
God is great, God is good   68
For our food and those who prepare it   68
Now my plate is full   69
Some ha'e meat and canna eat   69
When I call out, you will answer   74
Thank you for the firefighters   75
Thanks be to thee, O Lord Jesus Christ   119
Harvest time is gold and red   135
Let us thank God for Christmas   136
Good Friday is a time of sadness   150

## water
O most high, almighty, good Lord, God   12
Thank God for sleep in the long quiet night   22
Dear God, give us a flood of water   44
The bread is warm and fresh   67

God, we thank you for this food   64
We thank you, Lord, for happy hearts   65
Back of the bread is the flour   66
The Lord is good to me   66
Thank you for the firefighters   75
O Brother Jesus, who as a child was carried into exile   79
O Christ, you calm the storm at sea   92
You who guided Noah over the flood waves   93
As the rain hides the stars   98
Here on the ancient rock of earth   115
Sleep my little one! The night is all wind and rain   166
Praise the Lord! Praise the Lord from heaven   176

## winter

Summer sky of blue and white   15
Praise the Lord for all the seasons   27
Praise the Lord for all the beauty   28
Thank you very much indeed   29
Winter creeps   30
How many miracles you strike in spring, Lord   30
Come, ye thankful people, come   37
O thought I!   38
We thank you, loving Father God   40
We stood on the hills, Lady   140

## work

Thank you, God in heaven for a day begun   26
When I call out, you will answer   74
Thank you for the firefighters   75
You are the God of the poor   76

O Christ, you calm the storm at sea   92
You who guided Noah over the flood waves   93
Peace of the running waves to you   99

## weather

O most high, almighty, good Lord, God   12
Thank you for the sunshine bright   14
For dawn of grey and tattered sky   18
Morning has broken   20
Thank God for sleep in the long quiet night   22
Thank you, God in heaven for a day begun   26
Praise the Lord for all the seasons   27
Praise the Lord for all the beauty   28
Thank you very much indeed   29
Thank you, God, for sunshine   31
For buckets and spades, for sunshine and shade   32
I'll shut my eyes and pretend I can be   32
For all the rich autumnal glories spread   34
First the seed   37
Come, ye thankful people, come   37
O thought I!   38
God bless the field and bless the furrow   44
Dear God, give us a flood of water   44
Please God, take care of little things   48
For eyes whereby I clearly see   58

# Index of Authors

David Adam   78
Sue Aldridge   145
Cecil Frances Alexander   41
E.J. Allen-Williams   66, 68
Mary Anderson   27
Lancelot Andrewes   121
Angela Ashwin   102
Sir Jacob Astley   89
Dorothy E. Baker   79
Sabine Baring-Gould   162
Mary Batchelor   18, 31, 43, 47, 63,
   99, 102, 150
Henry Charles Beeching   59
G.W. Briggs   46, 55
Mike Brooks   69
Robert Browning   31
Robert Burns   69
William Canton   85
Amy Carmichael   91
John Cennick   68
John Chapman   66
Matthias Claudius   64
St Clement of Alexandria   116
Samuel Taylor Coleridge   42
George William Conder   13
Miles Coverdale   148
Lilian Cox   37
E.E. Cummings   16
Ralph Spalding Cushman   11
Susan Cuthbert   132
Percy Dearmer   30
Joyce Denham   92
Richard Molesworth Dennis   58
John Drinkwater   22
Mary L. Duncan   158
Mary S. Edgar   118
Emily E.S. Elliott   139
G.J. Elvey   37
Ralph Waldo Emerson   17
Eleanor Farjeon   20, 48
A.S.T. Fisher   64
St Francis of Assisi   12, 124
Maryleona Frost   64
Norman Gale   29
John Galsworthy   52
Phyllis Garlick   120
Carmen Bernos de Gasztold   44
Mizuno Genzo   61
Gilbert of Hoyland   112

Elizabeth Gould   28, 35
Louise Imogen Guiney   25
Rev. W.H. Havergal   159
Kumi Hayashi   60
Christopher Herbert   32, 57, 70, 71
Holling C. Holling   166
Hsieh Ping-hsin   111
Archbishop Trevor Huddleston   81
Bishop Thomas Ken   156
Brendan Kennelly   45
Timothy King   110
Margaret Kitson   72
Rajah Jacob   82
Emilie Fendall Johnson   65
Mary Joslin   15
Allen M. Laing   33
Elizabeth Laird   19
Edith Rutter Leatham   65
Jane Eliza Leeson   85
John Leland   154
St Ignatius Loyola   123
Martin Luther   158
Catherine Maccabe   137
Alistair MacLean   98
Walter John Mathams   85
Ena V. Martin   71
Norman and Margaret Mealey   133
Thomas Miller   160
Thomas More   121
Ali Newell   152
John Henry Newman   106
Marjorie Newman   56
Mary Osborn   36
John Oxenham   88
Kathleen Partridge   130
St Patrick   86, 100, 117
William Penn   71

Ianthe and Oliver Pratt   142
Sarum Primer   122
Richard of Chichester   119
Sarah Betts Rhodes   62
Lois Rock   45, 50, 96, 115, 135
Christina Rossetti   142
Hilda I. Rostron   40, 72
Agnes Sanford   32
Clive Sansom   140
Siegfried Sassoon   24
Fiona Satow   30
Albert Schweitzer   54
J.D. Searle   136
Robert Louis Stevenson   143
Jan Struther   86
Philip Tebbs   74
Victoria Tebbs   75
Mother Teresa of Calcutta   124
Joan Gale Thomas   73, 81, 84
Henry Twells   103
Jane Vansittart   101
Lynn Warren   50
H. Widdows   14
Elfreyda M.C. Wightman   155
Alison Winn   105
Dorothy Wordsworth   38

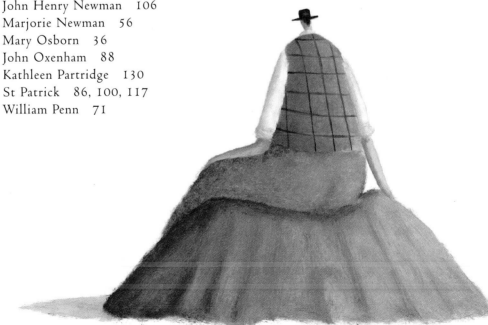

# Index of First Lines

Ah, dearest Jesus, holy Child   158
All good gifts around us   64
All is silent   111
All that we ought to have thought and have not thought   130
All things bright and beautiful   41
All things praise thee Lord most high!   13
Answer me now, Lord!   173
As our tropical sun gives forth its light   127
As the rain hides the stars   98
At even when the sun was set   103
Away in a manger, no crib for a bed   138
Back of the bread is the flour   66
Be present at our Table, Lord   68
Be thou a bright flame before me   83
Bless all the homeless ones   79
Bless this house which is our home   171
Blessed are you, Lord our God   67
Blessed be the name of Jesus   146
By and by all things must die   105
Christ be with me   100
Christ is now risen again   148
Christ, let me see You in others   78
Come into my soul, Lord   107

Come, ye thankful people, come   37
Create a pure heart in me, O God   191
Day is done   151
Dear Father, help us to love one another   201
Dear Father, who hast all things made   55
Dear God, be good to me   95
Dear God, give us a flood of water   44
Dear God, you are my shepherd   96
Dear Jesus, as a hen covers her chicks   162
Drive from me every temptation and danger   95
Each time we eat   69
Ever since I was a child   192
Father of all mankind, make the roof of my house   70
Father, take all the broken bits of our lives   133
First the seed   37
For all the rich autumnal glories spread   34
For buckets and spades, for sunshine and shade   32
For dawn of grey and tattered sky   18
For every cup and plateful   64
For eyes whereby I clearly see   58
For flowers that bloom about our feet   17
For food and friends and all God sends   68
For health and strength   67

For Morn, my dome of blue   24
For our food and those who prepare it   68
For the things that I've done wrong   133
For water-ices, cheap but good   33
Forgive me for the angry words   130
From ghoulies and ghosties   169
Give me food that I may live   84
Glory to Thee, my God, this night   156
God be in my head, and in my understanding   122
God bless Africa   81
God bless all those that I love   155
God bless the field and bless the furrow   44
God, give me strength to run this race   101
God is great, God is good   68
God of all our cities   73
God of the busy daytime   88
God our Father, Creator of the world   80
God our Father, who made us all   81
God, our loving Father, help us remember the birth of Jesus   143
God the Father, bless us   99
God, we thank you for this food   64
God, who created me   59
God who has made the daisies   47
God, who made the earth   62
God, who touchest earth with beauty   118
Good Friday is a time of sadness   150
Grandfather, look at our brokenness   129
Guard me by day   155
Harvest time is gold and red   135
He prayeth best   42

Hear us, Holy Father   84
Here on the ancient rock of earth   115
How did you make the rainbow   19
How great and wonderful are all your works   189
How I love you, Lord!   195
How many miracles you strike in spring, Lord   30
How much longer will you forget me, Lord?   190
I am only a spark   126
I believe in the sun even when it is not shining   98
I bind unto myself today   86
I can do nothing   61
I go forth today   117
I look around and the sun's in the sky   18
I look to the mountains   197
I love God's tiny creatures   46
I pray for the gift of love   200
i thank You God for most this amazing   16
I will not hurry through this day!   11
I'll shut my eyes and pretend I can be   32
It is not far to go   91
Jesus bids us shine   121
Jesus, friend of little children   85
Jesus keep us safe to-day   84
Jesus, tender Shepherd, hear me   158
Jesus, who healed the sick   102
Lead kindly light, amid the encircling gloom   106
Let our friendships be strong, O Lord   70
Let the darkness of night surround us   152
Let this day, O Lord   121
Let us thank God for Christmas   136

Like the ox that ploughs so straight  50

Lord, hang on to me  102

Lord, I have given up my pride  193

Lord Jesus Christ... fill us with your love  123

Lord Jesus Christ, Son of God  134

Lord Jesus, you taught us to let the little children come
   to you  104

Lord, keep us safe this night  154

Lord, make me an instrument of your peace  124

Lord of all hopefulness, Lord of all joy  86

Lord of the loving heart  120

Loving Father, hear my prayer  43

Loving Shepherd of Thy sheep  85

Matthew, Mark, Luke, and John  168

May the grace of the Lord Jesus Christ  203

May the love of God our Father  72

May your Holy Spirit brood  82

Morning has broken  20

Morning is here  64

Mountains are very still  110

Move our hearts with the calm  112

My body is paralysed  60

My soul magnifies you, my Lord  198

My tongue can taste all sorts of things  56

Nobody knows the trouble I see, nobody knows but Jesus  101

Now I lay me down to sleep  154

Now my plate is full  69

Now the day is over  162

Now the daylight goes away  159

O Brother Jesus, who as a child was carried into exile  79

O Christ, you calm the storm at sea  92

O God, help us not to despise  71

O God, make us children of quietness  116

O great Chief, light a candle within my heart  127

O Great Spirit, help me never to judge another  78

O heavenly Father, protect and bless  54

O Jesus, be the canoe that holds me up in the sea
   of life  95

O let us feel you very near  108

O Lord Jesus, stretch forth your wounded hands  80

O Lord, my Lord, how great you are in all the world  188

O Lord, thou knowest how busy I must be this day  89

O most high, almighty, good Lord, God  12

O thought I!  38

Only a fool would fail  45

Our Father in heaven  175

Our Father, who art in heaven  174

Peace be to this house  170

Peace of the running waves to you  99

Please God, take care of little things  48

Plenty of Grace  170

Praise God for the animals  50

Praise the Lord! Praise God in his Temple!  186

Praise the Lord for all the beauty  28

Praise the Lord for all the seasons   27
Praise the Lord! Praise the Lord from heaven   176
Preserve us, O Lord, while waking   90
Put love into our hearts, Lord Jesus   71
Sing a new song to the Lord!   187
Sleep, my child, and peace attend thee   172
Sleep my little one! The night is all wind and rain   166
Some ha'e meat, and canna eat   69
Space counts for nothing, Lord, with thee   72
Still, very still   109
Summer sky of blue and white   15
Teach us, Lord, to serve you as you deserve   123
Tennis racket, baseball bat   57
Thank God for sleep in the long quiet night   22
Thank you for hard work done   153
Thank you for the firefighters   75
Thank you for the sunshine bright   14
Thank you for the world so sweet   65
Thank you God for autumn days   36
Thank you, God, for sunshine   31
Thank you, God in heaven   26
Thank you very much indeed   29
Thanks be to thee, O Lord Jesus Christ   119
The bread is warm and fresh   67
The day is past, the sun is set   160
The little cares that fretted me   25
The Lord bless thee, and keep thee   202
The Lord is good to me   66
The Lord is my light and my salvation   194
The Magi journeyed far to find you   142
The quiet room is hushed in prayer   108
The things, good Lord, that we pray for   121
The whole bright world rejoices now   149
The year's at the spring   31
There are some old people whose lives are like autumn   71
Thou didst leave thy throne and thy kingly crown   139
To all the humble beasts there be   52
Us and this: God bless   68
We can do no great things   4, 124
We give them back to you, dear Lord   105
We have so much to thank you for   63

We pray, Lord, for the humble beasts   51
We pray, mighty God, for those who struggle   77
We stood on the hills, Lady   140
We thank thee, Lord, for happy hearts   65
We thank thee, Lord, for quiet upland lawns   35
We thank you, loving Father God   40
We went to the beach, where the waves were so wild   137
What can I give him, poor as I am?   142
When I am tempted to take the sloping track of laziness   132
When I call out, you will answer   74
When I lie down, I go to sleep in peace   203
When I see the birds go soaring   45
When in the night I sleepless lie   157
Who is this Jesus? Who can he be?   145
Winter creeps   30
You are the God of the poor   76
You are to me, O Lord   128
You are wise and loving   131
You who guided Noah over the flood waves   93